I woke up this morning to a beautiful sunrise. The orange hue made the tree tops appear to be silhouettes resembling black construction paper cut-outs one would find in an elementary classroom. There was a quiet peacefulness that promised a fresh new start. But, in my world, promises are never meant to be kept.

The smell of fresh coffee calls to me. The creamy, hot, dark liquid tastes just as good as it smells. I sink into the big blue overstuffed chair and enjoy watching the neighbor dog briskly scamper across the street looking for her BFF to come out and play. Anxious to join her friend, Jade whines to go out. As I open the door for her, I hear Riley make his way to the kitchen. I take a deep breath and feel my muscles stiffen. Reality is upon me. No matter how pretty the sunrise, wonderful the coffee, peaceful the morning – it is just a prelude to insanity.

Surviving the Chaos

Caregiving the Caregiver

Linda Bartee Doyne

Copyright © 2012 Author Name

All rights reserved.

ISBN-13: 978-1540478481
ISBN-10: 1540478483

DEDICATION

This book is dedicated to anyone who has ever lived with, cared for, and become the caregiver to an alcoholic, especially an end-stage alcoholic.

Table of Contents

WHERE AM I & HOW DID I GET HERE? 1
Live Til You Die 1

WHAT DO I DO NOW? 3
Put yourself as your top priority 3
Discover who you really are. 4
Learn to be happy. 4
Make a plan. 4
Get on with the business of living towards your own goals. 5
    The Alcoholic's Spouse 6
    A Flawed Plan 8

TIPS FOR MAINTAINING SANITY 11
Be a rational realist. 11
Take care of your physical health. 11
Take care of your mental health. 11
Keep your objectivity. 11
Maintain your own life. 11
Establish a support network. 12
Educate yourself about alcoholism. 12
Find enjoyable distractions. 12
Find the comedy. 12
Be sure to enjoy every sunrise and sunset. 12
    Sacrifices… 13

LEAVE OR STAY 17
    Leave or Stay? 19

OPTIONS 23
    Medicare – Not a Knight in Shining Armour 24

PHYSICAL WELL-BEING 27
    Stress – a ticket to the ER Resort 29

THE OBVIOUS – EXERCISE & DIET 33
EXERCISE 33
DIET 34
True Confessions… *35*
A WORD ABOUT THE FAMILY 37
My Uncle Hank *39*
FINANCIAL HEALTH 43
Have a budget 43
Budget Worksheet (Monthly) 45
Annual Expense Tracking Worksheet 46
Savings 46
Taxes 47
Prepare for the worst 47
In conclusion 48
Financial Pit of Despair *49*
Drunk Driving Bitch *51*
ACCEPTANCE 55
Your alcoholic is not going to stop drinking. 55
You are not responsible for his alcoholism 56
You cannot cure the alcoholic 56
Your goals do not match the alcoholic's. 56
No amount of love will make it any better. 56
You were born into this world as an individual. 57
You have the ability to make your own decisions. 57
Being happy is your decision and only yours. 57
A State of Mind… *58*

DISCOVER YOURSELF 61
- Who You Are 61
- What you are about 63
- Occupation: 63
- Making Time 65
- Current and Daily Time Sheets 67
- Personality Tests 69
  - *He's the sick one – not me* *70*

DETACHMENT 73
- *Dead? Alive?* *75*

CO-DEPENDENCE 79
- *Co-Dependent – A dirty word?* *81*

SUPPORT GROUPS 85

RESOURCES 89
- *Recovery For All* *90*

WHEN THE FAT LADY SINGS 95
..... 95
- *Til death do us part* *97*

MY FAVORITE BLOG POSTS 99
- *Jury Duty* *100*
- *How happiness feels* *103*
- *Bootstraps* *105*
- *Tuesday's Towel* *107*
- *I'm A Writer: My Husband Is An Alcoholic* *109*

ACKNOWLEDGMENTS

A very special thank you to

Michelle Griffin, Carolyn Hall and Wren Waters

CHAPTER 1

WHERE AM I & HOW DID I GET HERE?

> She always knew who she was,
> and she knew who she could never be,
> but the brokenness inside her
> kept her up to date on reality.
>
> She tried so hard to please others,
> she looked up to outstanding mothers,
> but no matter how hard she tried,
> at the end of the day
> she cried.
>
> Just because someone wears a smile,
> you might not see the denial,
> but trust when I tell you this,
> their life is not full of bliss.
>
> And although she sins as she judges,
> and she often tends to hold grudges,
> she judges herself more harshly
> than anyone will ever know.
>
> —Michelle Griffin

Alcoholism is sneaky. The disease progresses slowly until you end up feeling that you are at a point of no return. It's all very innocent. You stick with the alcoholic because he really "isn't that bad yet" and suddenly you realize that things are far worse than you imagined. It's the Frog Soup syndrome.

Frog Soup Recipe:

If you put a frog into a pot of boiling water, it will jump out immediately. If you put the frog in a pot of cold water and slowly bring the water to a boil – you'll end up with frog soup.

For me, each time Riley entered a detox program, he came home sober but in a little worse physical condition than he was. My hope was that he would be well enough to take care of himself and move out of my house. But instead he just became more and more unable to attend to his own needs. Putting him out now would be like throwing a cancer patient out on the street with nowhere to go. Now he is totally dependent on me for everything in his life.

There's a battle that goes on inside my head. It's like the angel on one should and the devil on the other. The angel says "Help him. He has no one else. It's the right thing to do." On the other hand, the devil says "Kick him out. He never treated you with respect. Make him suffer now." I understand both sides and I've consider doing both of those things. My moral compass always wins out and I take care of him the best I can. In the end, I still have to live with myself.

That's how most people with an alcoholic in their life end up being the caregiver. There are other ways to get to the caregiver designation. Children and siblings of alcoholics almost always want to help and care for a parent (or sibling) who cannot manage on their own. They may not live in the same house, but they keep a watchful eye on what's happening. They may help keep the house clean and healthy food in the pantry. All the extra attention ends up being care giving and that can mean the end of having a life of your own.

I've heard from care givers whose only focus is on how the alcoholic is doing. They almost always feel defeated and depressed. No matter how hard they try nothing seems to really work. It's unclear what they really want to accomplish because they've lost sight of the goal amidst all the chaos.

So here you are. You are now the "go-to" person for the alcoholic. You're the decision maker, financial manager, housekeeper, cook, etc. In short you are everything to the alcoholic. But who are you to you?

I certainly wouldn't tell you to stop being a care giver. That's a decision only you can make. However, I would like for you to consider a person who needs care and isn't getting any or enough. That person is YOU. You need You. You need to save your own life and step up for yourself.

And what if you don't? What if you continue to put all your energy into making sure the alcoholic is safe, comfortable and well fed? The alcoholic may very well out live you. You may suffer from stress-related illnesses and it only takes one to do you in forever. Who will take care of the alcoholic when you are gone? If you have children, who will take care of them if you walk off this earth early? In my opinion, it would be a real shame for the care giver to sacrifice his/her life so that the alcoholic could continue making others miserable. I suppose in that case, the alcohol would win the battle to control all those around.

That's where you are and that's how you got here. What are you going to do about it?

Live Til You Die
From Immortal Alcoholic blog post September 15, 2012

There is no way around it. No way to fight it or fend it off. Alcoholism destroys lives. It takes away free-will, rational thought and the ability to appreciate life in and of itself. Alcoholism is a slow form of suicide and it is painful for everyone around to watch as it progresses toward death.

Caregivers of end-stage alcoholics do everything and anything to keep the alcoholic from reaching death's door. They plead, manipulate, threaten, and anything else they think will help at the time. Many live insane lives trying to find some reason in the chaos. Is the whole process futile? Does a caretaker ever manage to really reach the alcoholic's sensibility to make a difference?

Maybe the process is futile. But, just maybe the one alcoholic that person is dealing with is the one that finally gets the fact that life is worth living. How are we to know if we don't try? And so we try. We try over and over again.

When I hear about people trying to find ways to prevent their alcoholic from getting the alcohol or from drinking their coveted juice, I get this little chill up the backside of my neck. Because even though I think we must try to help the alcoholic find reason, I also think there is a line that must be drawn about how much trying we should do.

In my opinion, it is not productive to file law suits against drinking establishments who serve alcohol to drunken patrons. It is also not productive to force cab drivers to refuse to take inebriated persons to the liquor store. Forcing others to be accountable for the bad decisions made by others is just too much policing for my taste.

There are other things that can be done. Calling the police and reporting that your drunken loved one has just driven off, for example, is one way to make the alcoholic's drinking life difficult. When they are in jail, don't bail them out. Don't call their employment and tell them the alcoholic is too sick to come into work. Don't clean up their messes. In short, let these people be responsible for their own actions. Make them accountable and don't back down on any consequences that have been established by either you or society. Of course that is just my opinion.

As most of us know, things change a lot as the alcoholic becomes end-stage. It becomes easier to just let them be the way they want rather than to try to initiate change in any manner. After several rehabs or detoxes, it becomes obvious nothing is going to stop them from making that journey to the morgue. It is inevitable. It may take days, weeks, months, years, but it will happen.

Once the reality hits that change in favor of the better life for the alcoholic is not going to happen, we must change our point of view and take a look at our own life. Of course, we should have been doing that all along – but – something happens and we get all tangled up in the drama. Some of us even begin to welcome the drama because it is an indicator that we are still alive. But, our lives are more important than that. Life is for the ones who truly want to live – I don't see end-stage alcoholics as people who really desire even one more year of life. It is the caregivers who want to live. Unfortunately, if they don't come to terms with that they will often die before the alcoholic from the sheer stress of the trying to preserve the alcoholic's unwanted life.

My mother was really big on saying that today was a wonderful day and that we will never have it back again. She insisted on productivity in each and every day. She never wasted one day – not ever. I'm a bit like her. I don't want to waste a day because I'll never have this day to do over again. Once it's gone – it's gone forever. I don't think I have to be productive work-wise every day, but I do have to produce something that is meaningful. I not only insist, but demand, that I find some joy in each day. I find humor in a simple word or action. I smile even when I want to frown. I find something to do that creates a good feeling inside me, even if no one else notices.

I'm lucky. I have found my passion. If it had not been for all the nonsense I've been through with being Riley's caretaker, I may not ever have known that my passion was helping others survive similar ordeals. Other people have other passions. For one woman it was taking photographs of her pets. Another enjoyed reading stories to children at the local library. These two women were trying to find a way to escape all the insanity and when they ventured out past the alcoholic world, they found life in the other worlds they explored.

No one knows better about how difficult a task it may be to step aside and let the alcoholic do as they are going to do. After all, we must protect ourselves and our homes from the damage they can create. Sometimes we must find a person who will stay in the house with the alcoholic while we are gone. Sometimes we have to close the door to their area while occupying ourselves with other activities. I've heard of one man who observed his alcoholic daughter over a period of time and made notes and videos of her decline. He then put together a video document. He also put together a memory book of all the great memories he had and wanted to remember forever. After the daughter's death, he put his alcoholic creation in her casket with the daughter. No one will ever see it. He keeps the memory book on a table within easy reach. Both creations (good and bad) occupied his time and thoughts and when it was over – he realized he had found a way for it to be truly over forever without losing all the good things his daughter represented. The time span for his creation was only about a year. It was a year well spent because he now has the rest of his life to be free.

As caregivers, we must not forget how to enjoy our own life. It is our responsibility to be as happy as we can possibly be. OK. So the alcoholic did something horrendous and we must now find a way around it or fix it or do SOMETHING about it. So do it and move on to the next challenge while finding a way to look forward to something that is pleasant for you. Do what you must that may be distasteful and immediately follow it with something that makes you smile. A few minutes ago I cleaned Riley's poop from the bathroom floor, now I'm here writing in my blog, because it makes me happy. Tomorrow after doing all his ugly laundry, I'll be taking a walk on the beach. This is how I survive.

Life as the caregiver of an end-stage alcoholic is never easy. Sometimes it feels downright impossible. But we must always remember that life is for those who WANT to live. It's not an easy thing to remember, especially if your alcoholic is your child. If we give up our lives for theirs, who will take care of them? So in a round-about-way, helping ourselves is also helping them.

CHAPTER 2

WHAT DO I DO NOW?

To some people the answer to that question may be obvious. But, what if you are in a situation where you can't stop caregiving the alcoholic. Maybe your livelihood depends on the alcoholic's income or maybe the alcoholic is just too sick and needs care. You can still take care of the alcoholic, but also take care of yourself.

> *Our lives are not determined by what happens to us but by how we react to what happens, not by what life brings us, but by the attitude we bring to life. A positive attitude causes a chain reaction of positive thoughts, events, and outcomes. It is a catalyst, a spark that creates extraordinary results.*
>
> *--Anonymous*

Put yourself as your top priority

No one needs you more than you do. What you want and need should be the most important thing going on for you. Whatever you do for the alcoholic must be done around YOUR time schedule rather than the alcoholic's. If you want to go for a jog before breakfast then do it. Don't wait and do it after you've prepared the alcoholic's breakfast. One thing will lead to another and you will find that you didn't get to jog at all.

I've always had trouble getting a morning shower in before bedtime. Once I go into my husband's room I get sidetracked by all the things that need to be done in there. Simply taking his coffee into him can turn into a 2 hour ordeal of cleaning and doing for him. So I stopped. I now get out of bed and go straight to the shower. I don't even make the coffee until I've showered and dressed.

Figure out what you want out of your life

If someone were introducing you, would you want that person to define you as "This is

Jennie Jones. She is a really great care giver to here alcoholic father." Or would you rather be introduced as the "best storyteller the library has ever had." Of course, in order to be the best storyteller, you must actually do the story telling.

The point is that you must find something you would like to do and then do it. You might want to go back to work; learn to decorate cakes; volunteer for the community performing group; write or edit books; or anything else that interests you.

> *I want you to be everything that's you, deep at the center of your being.*
> --Confucius

Discover who you really are.

Do some self-exploration and find out what you are passionate about. Find out what your hopes and dreams were before the days of care giving. Make a list. Combine this item with the #2 item and figure out who you would like to be. Then set a course to become that person.

You may have to go back to school. Great! Take one class so as not to overwhelm yourself with responsibility. Remember you still have a human at home who needs your attention. But, you can put your class first and work around caring for the alcoholic.

Don't under estimate the volunteer opportunities in your neighbor. Working as a volunteer allows you to get out of the house for a while and do something that someone will appreciate. In the course of volunteering, you may discover an unknown talent. You might be able to turn that volunteer job into a money making endeavor.

Learn to be happy.

Happiness is really just a state of mind. The alcoholic will test you and try to drive that happiness right out of you. That's because misery loves company. Don't accept the invitation to the alcoholic's party.

You have a lot to be thankful for in this very moment. You woke up this morning. You have a plan to continue your day in a productive (for you) manner. There are opportunities on the horizon. Remember it takes less muscles to generate a smile than it does to frown. Besides, has being miserable EVER really gotten you anything that you really want? I doubt it.

Make a plan.

Actually, you should be making several plans. There should be one for the day, and one for each year as they go by. At the day's end, you can congratulate yourself on sticking to your course. You can feel good about it and be happy for what you accomplished. At the end of the year, you can look back and do the same thing.

Get on with the business of living towards your own goals.

Keep putting one foot in front of the other until you are where you want to be. Remember that your goal is to be happy in spite of what the alcoholic is doing.

The Alcoholic's Spouse
From Immortal Alcoholic blog August 28, 2016

I'm not an alcoholic. In some circles that statement would be considered a denial of being an alcoholic when I actually am an alcoholic. In that circle I would be damned either way. Logic tells me I'm not an alcoholic. I drink a glass or two of wine every year. I don't over-indulge. I haven't been drunk since I went to Jimmie's place for a protest party in 1967. I know I'm not an alcoholic.

I also know that alcohol has damaged my life. Being the wife of an alcoholic has caused me to be someone that I never wanted to me. I can turn into a shrew in an instant. I am less social and less trusting. Where I was once at the top of my game professionally, I stopped being able to concentrate on my office work. I used to be outgoing and friendly with a positive attitude. Now I just want to be left alone. My once balanced budget is now a sea of red. Even when I have money, I'm hesitant to spend it for fear of having none.

At the time I took Riley back in, my life was happy, independent, free and open to meet new people. That all changed after his first near-death encounter just a few weeks after he came to my house to stay. My friends stopped coming around. It was harder for me to work. I was spending all my savings on things I needed to care for him. There didn't seem to be anything left over for nails, hair or restaurant gatherings.

I kept taking care of him because I was told by medical professionals that he was dying. I fell into a frog soup situation. Each time he recovered from a near fatal situation, his health was worse. He could not take care of himself – and now he is completely bedridden. And here I am still acting as his caregiver.

Something is different now than when I first started caring for him. I have found my life again. I work at what I want to do and don't let Riley's condition stand in my way. Well… that may be an exaggeration… but I'm getting closer everyday to spending more time away from him.

When I started this blog way back in 2010 I found my passion or more accurately, I rekindled my passion for writing. I became more active on FaceBook and re-connected with old friends. I took every opportunity to smile and talk to complete strangers on the street, in the grocery story, and everywhere I went. I came back to life as through I had been asleep for a long time.

As typical with lives, mine ebbed and waned as problems and situations changed. Riley got worse or

better. We moved several times. I got sick. I got well. It's called life. Even when I lost focus on my life, I knew I was in there just waiting for the opportunity to get out.

That's what it is being the spouse

of an alcoholic. It's a constant struggle to remain alive and not disappear into his chaos. It's so easy to stop thinking or doing for yourself because you become absorbed by the alcoholic. There are messes to clean up and things to be done that would normally be the responsibility of the alcoholic. You cease having a personality of your own. Your image to the outside world is that of a weak, clingy, victim who is the alcoholic's slave and aid to his disease. No spouse would really want that but that's part of being in the frog soup pot.

Frog Soup – Put a frog into a pot of boiling water and it will jump right out. Put the frog in a pot of cold water and slowly bring the water to a boil. The frog will stay in the pot and become Frog Soup.

The changes in the alcoholic household happen slowly and are nearly unrecognizable until the situation boils over. Once the alcoholic becomes so sick or dependent, the spouse becomes the caregiver and if she/he is not careful, they lose their life while still breathing.

It is very important for the spouse to remain the person that they want to be. If you find you're losing it – search within yourself for what ignites your own passion. It takes some work in handling the details with the alcoholic. But it can be done. Don't let the alcoholic's desire to live in chaos become your existence. Create, generate, and/or preserve your own circle of friends. There are ways to meeting people in your situation other than Al-Anon, however, Al-Anon is a good start.

If it's early in the disease, make plans for getting out. You may not want to go right now, but in the future, it may be the safest thing for you to do. Keep your options open.

No matter what… remember that you are a person worthy of a life of your own filled with peace, happiness, and independence.

A Flawed Plan
From Immortal Alcoholic blog dated October 22, 2011

The Plan

My plan is always to just let him go. Let the alcoholic come to its inevitable final conclusion. He will bleed internally and I will ignore the nosebleeds and weeping scabs on his arms and legs. I will pay no attention to the fact that he eats only spoonfuls of food that have often have been from a 3 week old leftover that has been hidden in the back of the fridge. When he stumbles over his own feet, falls down and loses control of his bladder, I will let him lie in his filth until he figures out for himself how to regain a vertical stance and clean up the mess. Well… that's the plan…

The Flaw

The First Law of Robotics: A robot cannot cause the harm of a human or through inaction allow a human to come to harm.

In order to adhere to the plan I can no longer view this alcoholic as a human being or remember that he is the father of my children or a person that I once loved and would lie down my life to protect. I must view this person as one who is not deserving of medical attention and or any attempt at preserving his physical life.

I don't know how to do what I must do in order to fulfill the plan because to not care about a human life; to not make every attempt at prolonging or saving a life; feels somehow immoral. Although I'm not the epitome of virtue, I just cannot, in essence cause a person's death by reason of non-action. For some reason, I feel I must adhere to the first law of robotics.

Maybe I'm not really a human, maybe I'm a robot that was built specifically for this alcoholic. Was there something my parents had neglected to tell me??

CHAPTER 3

TIPS FOR MAINTAINING SANITY

The caregiver must take special care to prevent burn-out and health issues related to stress. Unfortunately, the caregiver often will display symptoms of stress-related disorders long before the alcoholic reaches the end. As a caregiver, I live by a certain set of standards that helps me keep things in perspective and give me a better life. I've listed them here.

> *The definition of craziness is when you drink the poison and wait for the other person to die.*
> --Author Unknown

Be a rational realist.

You did not cause the alcoholism. You cannot cure it. There are only two ways out – sobriety or death. In the case of end-stage alcoholism, this is a terminal illness.

Take care of your physical health.

Stress of caregiving an alcoholic can lead to health issues for the caregiver. It is not uncommon for the caregiver to have heart issues, hypertension, and stroke, and/or develop asthma and/or insomnia. Go to your medical doctor regularly for check-ups, flu shots, etc.

Take care of your mental health.

Find a therapist that has experience with caregivers of alcoholics. This can help you keep your perspective.

Keep your objectivity.

It's not your illness. The end-stage alcoholic is no longer the person you fell in love with or took care of you as a child. That person is gone and has been replaced by the pod people leaving you with a person you don't recognize. Grieve the loss, feel the hurt – when you do that the worst is over.

Maintain your own life.

End-stage alcoholics take a lot of time away from everyone else in the household because they have to be monitored for everyone's protection. That doesn't mean the caregiver should stop doing the things they love. Find a person who can stay with the alcoholic while you do whatever it is you want to do. If the alcoholic can still be left at home alone – take advantage of it. Focus on your passion -- quilting, scrapbook, cooking, painting, writing, woodworking, being musical. Let your passion be your escape.

Establish a support network.

These systems are everywhere. Besides the standard Al-Anon (which doesn't always fit for the end-stage caregiver), there are forums on sites such as about.alcoholism.com or soberrecovery.com, blogs written by people who have been caregivers, personal friends and family. Develop and nurture these relationships because they will give you someone to vent to, other than your therapist.

Educate yourself about alcoholism.

Knowledge is the key to survival. The more you know the more you will find surviving easier. Search the web, ask questions from others. Do your homework. It won't save the alcoholic, but it will fill up that space in your brain that is always whispering – what if…

Find enjoyable distractions.

When the alcoholic is just raging about this or that, or if he's spilled his drink for the 50th time today, take a mental break. I love the old commercial that goes – Calgon, take me away! So I fill up the tub with lots of bubbles and spend a little time in some imaginary place far away. Sometimes I only get 15 minutes – but its 15 minutes that can restore my sanity.

Find the comedy.

It's everywhere. Even the most serious of events can have a humorous side. Alcoholism is an absurd condition associated with outlandish actions. Have ever said – if it wasn't so sad, it would be funny? Well take out the "sad" and just make it funny. Laugh. Laugh as often as you can and for as long as you can. You will feel better for it.

Be sure to enjoy every sunrise and sunset.

Sacrifices...
From Immortal Alcoholic Blog, July, 28, 2011

A friend told me she went on a little week-end vacation to a place that's just a couple hours from her house. She left her alcoholic husband at home. He is NOT end-stage, but he is heading in that direction. At about 1 a.m. on the first night, he called because he had passed out in the driveway and was too drunk to get into the house. She called her son who lived down the street. He rushed out to help his father.

When she told me about it I said... **What??? You woke up your son to take care of his father who was in a drunken state??** *I don't know about you... but it seems to me, the alcoholic was sober enough hit all the right tiny little buttons on the phone... surely he could manage putting his keys into the door locks. Oh... he was too drunk to walk?? Was he too drunk to crawl??*

This, in my opinion, is a case of the non-alcoholics taking away an opportunity for the alcoholic to face the consequences of his own actions.

If it had been me in that situation, I would have told him that he would have to figure it out for himself. I would have left him in the driveway. I know he would call every 5 minutes, but I would have turned my phone off. I know the neighbors would call the police when they saw him passed out in the driveway and I'm thankful for their concern. I would have nothing to be embarrassed about because I was not the one passed out in the driveway.

Of course, the next day, the alcoholic remembered very little of what had transpired the night before. So what did he learn – nothing. If he had awakened in the driveway – he might have learned something. If he never has to face how bad his drinking is, how will he ever understand how bad it is? There are consequences, but his wife and son didn't allow him to have any because they removed them. Therefore, the consequences went to the wife – who spent her first night away worrying about her husband – and the son – who got out of his nice warm bed to physically get his father into the house. For the husband there was no consequence and no bad memory. **How can that be right?**

The wife and son must learn detachment. This is the only way we non-alcoholics can continue to have a life of our own. Detachment frees us from the chaos created by the alcoholic's unreasonable demands. It also frees us from the fear that anyone who knows us will lump us into a package deal of insanity. It's hard to not care about what others think – it's almost unnatural. But, non-alcoholics must develop a thick skin and the ability to separate personas. If a neighbor asks about the incident, a response such as "Well, yes, it's unfortunate that he drinks so much. Thank you for your concern." But, don't take ownership of the drunk's actions. You did nothing wrong – you have nothing to be ashamed of or to have to explain.

In another case, a woman's very end-stage mother lives with her. The mother is classic in that she sleeps in the day and is awake most of the night. The mother wakes up the daughter throughout the night making it impossible for the daughter to sleep. The daughter gets up and makes the mother a drink hoping it will be enough to get the mother to go back to sleep. The daughter knows she must sleep, but can't ignore her mother's calls for her to join her.

I believe, somewhere in the alcoholic haziness, it may be how they can have control of something in their lives. They have no control over the alcohol, but they can control what the non-alcoholic does be using the fear that something may be wrong. So when the alcoholic calls out, we respond because the alcoholic might be physically hurt and in need of assistance. Maybe it's not the complicated. Maybe it's as simple as the alcoholic is miserable and misery loves company that is also miserable.

If I were the daughter, I would firmly tell the alcoholic that I am going to bed now and do not wake me up. I would put a note someplace where the alcoholic would see it – do not wake me up. Then, because the alcoholic will ignore the notes, when she calls to me, I would call back asking what she wants. If she is not in peril, I would tell her I was not coming to help her. After that, I would lock my door, turn on my sleep music and attempt to go back to sleep. She will call again because she has no short-term memory. But, I would not respond. I might not be able to go back to sleep, but I would stay in my room and let her do whatever she is going to do. Once the pattern is established that I will not come to her in the middle of the night – maybe she will stop calling out. It might take a few nights for the message to sink in. If she doesn't stop, maybe I will get used to it and be able to ignore it.

If that scenario doesn't work and the alcoholic is still interrupting the non-alcoholic's sleep, I think I would do my best to hire someone to come in and spend four to six hours a night with the alcoholic. In essence, get a baby-sitter. Even four hours of uninterrupted sleep is better than eight hours with intermittent ups and downs.

*As non-alcoholic's we sacrifice ourselves for the safety of the alcoholic. The wife sacrificed her vacation, the daughter sacrificed sleep. But, the sacrifice doesn't serve us well. We gain nothing except frustration when we run to the rescue of those who refuse to rescue themselves. I know that the caregivers of end-stage alcoholics must do the task of "taking care." But, if we don't **take care** of ourselves there won't be anyone left to do the caregiving of the alcoholic.*

CHAPTER 4

LEAVE OR STAY

It's very easy for those around you to tell you what you must do. Sometimes if you don't follow their advice, they become angry and may even end your relationship. What these people don't understand is that there is more to the question of leaving and staying than they realize. Both answers, leave or stay, create problems on their own. The question is which set of problems are easier to deal with in the long term.

There is a movie named "A Simple Plan" starring Bill Paxton, Billy Bob Thornton, Brent Briscoe and Bridget Fonda. Bill and Billy Bob find a downed airplane with a dead pilot and loads of cash. They come up with a simple plane where they keep the airplane and its contents a secret. As time goes on the *simple* plan becomes complicated.

> *If your house catch on fire,*
> *And there ain't no water round*
> *Throw your trunk out the window*
> *Let your house burn down...*
>
> *--Unknown songwriter*

That's the way things seem to go when making plans. If you plan to leave their will be repercussions and consequences. Your plan to simply go, don't look back, or kick him to the curb, change the locks, will need planning which may be complicated. The same goes for staying. It doesn't matter which way you choose, it will be complicated and it will be messy.

Because you are reading this book, you are probably past the point of making a decision to either leave or stay. If the alcoholic is at end-stage, you probably feel a moral obligation to see the alcoholic through to the end. This book is really about flourishing in spite of that decision. But I want to cover this subject for anyone who has not yet made the decision.

Reasons for people leaving the alcoholic are obvious. Drunken alcoholics are unpleasant, demanding, and can often be dangerous. If you have very young children you probably don't want them exposed to the bad behavior. The problems that may be incurred after leaving can include things like, where to live, how to support yourself and your kids. To leave the plan must be clear and easy to follow.

Often times the non-alcoholic leaves but stays close enough to keep a watchful eye on the alcoholic. Without being a party to the actions, they can monitor food intake and make sure the alcoholic is not in a dangerous environment. That situation helps the non-alcoholic feel comfortable about the decision.

I understand staying with the alcoholic. There may be children who have reached an age that having the alcoholic gone would be more complicated than if the drunkenness were front and center. Maybe the alcoholic hasn't yet progressed to the point of being too obnoxious. If the alcoholic is functional, that is, still working and being a productive member of the household, it may be best for all concerned to stay.

Even if you stay, you must be preparing a plan to leave because someday the alcoholic will leave. Whether it be mentally or physically – they are going to leave. Eventually death will be the cause of leaving. It may take a long time for that exit, but eventually it will happen.

The trick is to not let yourself get caught in the frog soup syndrome and end up in a place where you have little choice. Figure out what you're going to do and begin making your plans and alternative plans now while things are less chaotic. Don't bother to discuss your plan with the alcoholic. He/she really doesn't care about your plans. The plans are clear for the drinker – they plan to drink for as long as they are capable of raising the glass/bottle to their lips. There is no plan for them to stop.

Leave or Stay?
Immortal Alcoholic blog page

My first presentation in a series was titled "Leave or Stay??" The presentation included the 12 Stages of Alcoholism and was focused on alcoholism in general. For this posting, I'm focusing only on end-stage alcoholism. I can't post the entire presentation – but – below is the Cliff Notes version:

So – leave or stay? That is the question. No one can really answer that question except the non-alcoholic faced with the dilemma of having to make a choice. I'm big on making sure I am thoroughly familiar with an issue before I make decisions – especially life altering ones. Knowing what to expect is the best place to start.

We all know that alcoholism is a pain in the patutti. But when the alcoholic becomes "end-stage" the difficulties become compounded by about a 100 times – or at least it seems so to the other people in the alcoholic's household.

You can expect the alcoholic do display some of the traits below:

1. Loss of interest in family, friends, hobbies and anything outside of being drunk.

2. Loss of memory – mostly short-term, but can also affect long-term. There will be confusion between which day starts and which day ends.

3. Reversed or erratic sleeping cycle. The alcoholic will spend more and more daytime hours sleeping and may be up and roaming the house during the night.

4. Personal hygiene becomes non-existent or selective and very difficult. Usually showing requires the insistence of an outside party. Assistance while in the shower is often necessary. Shaving is problematic if the alcoholic doesn't use an electric razor.

5. Inabilities for blood to clot making even the simplest scratch require immediate attention. Nosebleeds increase in frequencies and intensity.

6. Falls easily and has difficulty getting up even when assisted by another person. Since there is a loss of muscle mass, there is no strength to hold onto to the person attempting to help.

7. Loss of bladder and bowel control. The alcoholic will frequently urinate without even realizing that he is doing so. Bowel movements will become diarrhea-like and often the alcoholic will not be able to hold it until he gets to the toilet. A diaper may be necessary -- but it may be difficult to get the alcoholic to agree. Protective pads must be used on all the alcoholic's favorite furniture places and in the bed.

8. Vomiting gradually increases to a daily occurrence.

9. Makes unreasonable demands of the caregiver and/or the family and will become hostile when he doesn't have his demands met. Or, after the caregiver and family do everything possible to meet the demand – the alcoholic doesn't remember ever making the demand.

10. Easily irritated, angered and may possibly morph a quiet peaceful person into a violent rage-filled bully.

11. Loss of appetite. Although he may say he's hungry, he will only eat a few bites of food at any sitting. Then he may pick at various foods throughout the day. Or he may stop eating altogether.

12. Loss of appropriate social behavior and inhabitation. Anything goes. Everything is acceptable in the alcoholic's mind. There are no morals and no shame.

13. He may become insistent that there is something wrong with him – cancer – bird flu – plague – anything that is not alcohol related. And he will either be very insistent upon seeing a doctor or will refuse and just keep complaining.

If you think you might stay, you must know that dealing with all the above issues is time-consuming and stressful. Cleanliness will be of the upmost importance for you and your family. The alcoholic will leave in his disheveled, filthy wake, the possibly of exposing everyone to salmonella and other bacterial infections. Here are some things to consider:

1. Use latex gloves and protective masks when handling any of the articles of clothing or bedding whether or not they contain excrement.

2. When cleaning the alcoholic's bathroom, use a solution of 1 part bleach to 2 parts water. Clean the toilet daily, but also clean the floor and walls behind the toilet.

3. Put waterproof pads between the sheets and mattress.

4. The alcoholic's laundry must be done separate from the family laundry. The alcoholic's laundry must be done at least every other day.

5. Keep a very small trash can by his bed. Use a plastic can liner – doubled. He can use this if he needs to vomit and can't get to the bathroom. Empty and clean each day using the bleach mixture.

6. Don't allow him to handle any food. Prepare his meals. If he eats during the night, prepare food and snacks that he can eat while you're sleeping. There's no point in designating breakfast from dinner. He can't make that leap – so just fix what you know he will like.

7. There is a "point of no return" where taking the alcohol away is just as dangerous as the drinking itself. So if the alcoholic cannot get to the store to buy his booze, you will need to decide on whether to buy it or not to buy it. Either choice is encouraging his death and puts the caregiver in a moral dilemma. Please see my post "To Buy or Not to Buy" posted in December 2010.

Now that you know a bit about what to expect and some of what may be required to keep him at home, here are your options:

1. Kick him out and he will die possibly within weeks of his exit.

2. Keep him in your house where you can provide a safe place for his deterioration. His life expectancy is probably ranging in months rather than years, although I've heard of alcoholics hanging on as long as two years in an end-stage state.

Those are really the only two options. The reasons WHY you leave or stay are really not as important as what you do after you make the decision.

If your decision is to take care of the alcoholic, you must also take care of yourself. Establish your own support system. Al-Anon is great, but often their tenements conflict with what you find you must do. But, there is a sense of acknowledgment of your pain and conflict. They will not judge. They will not advise.

I've found that developing my own support system works best for me. I have a friend (who has had issues with drugs and alcohol), my family, a mental health counselor, a medical doctor, a selective on-line Al-Anon group, my OARS Facebook and OARS Family Support websites.. Most importantly, all the readers of this blog. I consider these people collectively as my support group.

CHAPTER 5

OPTIONS

A part of your plan for the future may be to place the alcoholic into a care facility. That's an excellent idea. It's what I wanted to do with my alcoholic until I realized that it is very costly and way above my budgetary limits.

If a person has been in the hospital for a specific amount of time, the patient may go to a nursing/convalescent/physical rehabilitation center for a period of six weeks. In some circumstances the patient may stay longer but depends on meeting many varied requirements. After the six weeks the patient is discharged home or to some other living situation as the expense of the patient.

Medicare does not pay for any type of long-term care facility. These facilities usually cost upwards of $5000 per month and some require a large entrance fee. Let me repeat – Medicare does NOT pay for any type of long-term care facility.

> **There is no prince on a white steed and there is no cavalry riding in to the rescue. You're on your own.**
>
> --Immortal Alcoholic's Wife

Medicaid may pay for a facility but to qualify for Medicaid you must be nearly destitute. A person who brings in $1,200 a month most likely makes too much money to qualify. If you own your home, have stocks or bonds, or any other type of assets, you may be asked to liquefy all of them and use those funds prior to receiving Medicaid.

The Veterans Administration offers long-term care for veterans who have a military related disability with a rating of more than 70%. Otherwise, they only offer Hospice In-Patient care at the very end of the veterans life expectancy. It may take five or more years to apply for the veterans benefits and most first-time appliers are usually declined. These declined vets must apply for an appeal with takes about two years. If you believe your alcoholic might be eligible for veteran's benefits, you must start applying long before you actually need long-term care. Don't wait. Start the process today. Consult with a VA counselor right away. You may use the counselors at your local American Legion or Disabled American Veterans organization. This counseling should be free of charge.

If you go into caregiving an alcoholic knowing that Big Brother is not going to offer you any help, you are better prepared to make a plan that relies only on what you know you can do.

Medicare – Not a Knight in Shining Armour
From Immortal Alcoholic blog dated November 4, 2016

There is some confusion within the general population of our country. The confusion is that it is easy to place a person into a facility. Nothing could be further from the truth unless you are extremely wealthy or planned well for you golden age back when you were rockin' with Dick Clark.

Let me make this perfectly clear, Medicare does NOT pay for any type of long-term care in a facility. There are certain cases where they will cover up to six-weeks of care after a 3-day hospital stay. Let me say it one more time – DON'T expect Medicare to help pay for a nursing home for your mother or anyone else.

If you have worked throughout your life and collect Social Security benefits of about $1,200 - $1,400 per month, you probably make too much money to be accepted into the Medicaid program. So they will not pay for a nursing home facility. However, if you have been on welfare or aid for a large majority of your working years, you may not make enough on Social Security to eliminate you from qualifying for Medicaid. I am still trying to figure that one out.

You can qualify for Medicaid if you have enough "spend down" expenses, which you deduct from your income, to put you within range of acceptance. Expenses like paying for a personal aide or medical equipment can all be deducted from your total income. That's good to know.

If you are a Veteran, the VA will pay for a facility for you if you have a 70% disability rating on a military injury. Getting qualified and accepted with a disability percentage can take years to achieve. By the time you are qualified, the applicant may be dead and no longer in need of a facility.

Many people believe that Medicare will take care of us. Let me assure you, no one is riding in on a beautiful steed with a silver sword to come to your rescue. You will not be saved from the oncoming train. You're on your own and that's just the way it is.

If you were smart back in the 70s (when you were young enough to afford it), you bought long-term care insurance. That's about the only way you can pay for a nursing home without the entire amount coming from your pocket.

The cost of a long-term facility these days runs from $5K to about $9K per month depending on your location and the services required. Even if you planned well for your retirement, most people don't have that much extra cash available.

Riley and I worked from the time we were 14 years old. We have seldom been unemployed. We have both been known to work more than one job at a time. We have paid our taxes and have an above average retirement income. But it is not enough to support me and pay for a facility. In fact, the cost of a facility is more than the grand total of our income. Unfortunately, a social worker once told me that we'd be better off if we had not worked so hard. I apologize for our strong work ethic.

The bottom line is this… start planning now and put that plan into action. Figure out where you will live and who will care for you should you become unable to care for yourself. Meet with an Estate Attorney and get some legal advice about what is possible and what is just a dream. Get your ducks in a row now while you are still sane enough to make the hard decisions.

CHAPTER 6

PHYSICAL WELL-BEING

In order to enjoy your life, you must first have a life to enjoy. It is often said that the caregivers become physically sicker than the patient. It is vital that the person immersed in the alcoholic chaos get the proper medical attention and put their own health before the alcoholic's.

> *Our bodies are our gardens to which our wills are gardeners.*
>
> *--William Shakespeare*

You may think you are perfectly healthy and have had no medical complainants for a long time. But, have you been monitoring your blood pressure? Had a CBC blood test? Had your vision checked? These things and others can all be affected by the stress level you are experiencing.

A simple upset stomach can turn into a three-day stay in the hospital with a bacterial infection. A bladder infection may turn out to be a reason for a stent to become a necessity. Those headaches that seem to come at the end of the day is a red flag.

Lack of sleep is also a means to turn any little condition into a big problem. Combine sleeplessness with stress and you know have a lethal cocktail.

The first thing you must do is get in to your primary care physician and get a through wellness check-up. A few days before the appointment, keep a log of anything that bothers you. For example, if you have a headache write down specifics about the headache, where on your head is it? Is it sharp or dull pain? What would you consider the pain level to be? How long did it last? Did you take anything for relief and if so, what did you take?

I've included a form for tracking your physical aches and pains. You can take this form with you to the doctor's to give him a better understanding of what is going on with you and you won't have to remember it all.

Make sure you can get a copy of your medical record for the appointment and a copy of the lab report. You can use these items to track your own health status.

If the doctor comes back and says you have a condition that needs to be treated, make sure you put that condition as your top priority. If he/she says your healthy, then let's keep it that way by doing some preventative care like watching your diet and getting daily exercise.

Name

Address and Phone Numbers
Emergency Contact Information

MEDICAL HISTORY

PREVIOUS DIAGNOSIS

Year	Diagnosis	Comments

CURRENT MEDICATION LIST

Medication	Dosage	Frequency	For

IMMUNIZATIONS LIST

Date	Type

SURGICAL / OTHER PROCEDURES

Year	Procedure	Comments / Results	Location / Hospital

FAMILY HISTORY

Relative	Age	Condition	Medical Conditions

CURRENT PHYSICIANS

Name	Specialty	Phone

CURRENT HOUSEHOLD MEMBERS

Relationship	Comments

Stress – a ticket to the ER Resort
From Immortal Alcoholic blog dated June 7, 2016

Off and on over the past year, I've had intestinal issues. I would get sick for a day and then get better. Once I felt more "normal" I would simply forget about the brief encounter with an uncomfortable tummy and go about my caregiving duties.

A couple of Sundays ago, I woke up in such pain that I could hardly move around. I couldn't possibly take care of Riley because I couldn't even stand up. I called hospice to see about getting some help and they immediately found a bed for him in a nursing home. I thought I would just rest and go with the sickness to let it work itself out. After all, I thought, it is probably just a flu bug going around. I spent that Sunday on the sofa with a barf bag and the porta potty close by.

By Monday, I was worse. I was dizzy and kept trying to drink water, but it would not stay down. I called my doctor and he insisted I go to the emergency room. I said to myself, "Self, this could be a good thing. They'll fill me up with fluids, give me some meds, and send me home. Easy peasy." Off to the hospital I went.

Things weren't as "easy peasy" as I thought they would be. I was admitted to the heart observation unit because, evidently, dehydration can cause complications to the heart and kidneys. I am also diabetic and that was another concern. So I figured to just go with whatever the medical staff felt was best for me. Riley would be in respite until Sunday evening. If I needed to be in the hospital, now would be the time to stay at Riverside Resort (Riverside Regional Medical Center).

I was given a milky white drink that was supposed to taste like mint – a Berry-yum Cocktail. I was disappointed there was no slice of fruit or paper umbrella. It didn't taste too bad. Then I went to get my insides a tan using a CT Tanner (Scanner). The pictures showed nothing unusual – no blockage or twisting or anything else.

It doesn't add to your discomfort to be able to watch the good looking doctors, especially Dr. Franklin, scurry around to treat other resort (ER) clients. There was a constant influx of firemen and other first responders. I fell in and out of sleep as chaos of multiple traumas surrounded me.

Once in the observation unit, I met my team who would be taking care of me. I was hooked up to monitors and more bags of fluid were hung high on a pole. The nurses and attendants were extremely attentive and answers to my call were as close to immediate as possible. I am grateful to them all, especially Megan. Thank you for taking such good care of me.

The doctor in charge of my case was Dr. C – just "C" because his name was too hard to pronounce. He was tall, dark and handsome. More importantly he spoke to me in a language that I could understand. He had in tow, three other "younger" doctors who listened to his words like they held the key to some magic formula that would cure me of awful bug.

The doctor in the group that was assigned to oversee my care was Dr. Sylvia Le. At first I thought she had to be no more than 17 years old, but I was wrong. Dr. Le knew her stuff and answered every one of my questions without hesitation. I was impressed that she wanted to know about ME – who I am, what I do and how I got admitted to the hospital. She let me tell my story while giving me bits and pieces about her life. I felt connected to this woman. I was confident that she could treat me in the best possible manner. I listened to her advice me and explain to me how things got so bad.

There were three things that led to me being in the hospital. I had chronic viral gastritis (stomach flu) that worsened over time due to stress (primarily), but further complicated by allergies and diabetes. I got it months back but never recovered from it fully so each time it popped up, the symptoms were worse.

Stress – how many times have I heard that? 100 billion, at least. The responsibilities of caregiving Riley create the inability to really take a break to rest and recharge my batteries. I go through each day with changing his underwear, cooking three meals, keeping his room and body clean, giving him his meds, and retrieving anything he has dropped on the floor. I know it's not an easy job, but I've gotten so used to it that it is almost second nature to me and I don't notice that I'm beat to the bone. On top of that is the emotional stress of having to put him first. It's way too much.

Once my heart was determined to be A-OK, I was moved to D-Unit where Rebecca, Sarah and Rachel looked after me. They pampered, scolded, teased, and took care of all my needs.

I was finally given real food on Friday evening and it seemed to go and stay down as it should. On Saturday, I was sent home with instructions to get plenty of rest. It was clear that some changes must be made in order for me to stay healthy. Those changes are in the process.

CHAPTER 7

THE OBVIOUS – EXERCISE & DIET

EXERCISE

I have a gym membership. I'm not saying I use it a lot, but I do have one. I go there and watch all the perfectly physically fit people go about their exercise routines. I think to myself that it's disgusting to see all those gorgeous bodies work like crazy to achieve what they already have. Then I realize that they are probably going to eat dessert tonight while I will be eating a serving of Diet Jello. OK. I forgive them.

> If exercise is so good for you, why does the average athlete retire by the age of 35?
>
> --Unknown

Sometimes I get on the elliptical, but most time I just swim laps. It's a relaxing form of exercise. While going up and down the pool, I imagine that I'm somewhere tropical without the alcoholic anywhere around. I gather my thoughts and dream big dreams. It's my little place of peace and quiet.

It's common knowledge that exercise is great for the body, but it's also good for the soul. If I'm angry with the alcoholic, I can run away from him when I'm on the treadmill; climb out of his reach on the stair stepper; or kick him in the imaginary face when kick boxing. There's nothing wrong with getting out your aggressions while working those muscles. It's better than going home and committing a crime that will send you to jail.

Let's face it. I'm not big on exercise except swimming. I find it difficult to go to the gym and complete an exercise routine. But, I do exercise.

I walk around my property. If I lived in town, I'd be walking around the block or to the library. I do other common ordinary things that most people wouldn't consider to be formal exercise. I sweep the floors; do the laundry; climb the stairs; and all the other everyday things around the house. Grocery shopping is a big exercise for me because I walk up and down every aisle and make several back-tracks to get what I forgot. I unload the groceries and carry the heavy bags into the house. Grocery shopping generates a lot of exercise.

DIET

Personally, I try to stick to a low-carb food program. I said LOW carb and not zero carb. I try to keep my carbs under 40g per day. Of course I lose weight with this routine, but more importantly I feel awesomely energetic.

That's what works for me and may not work for you. You must find your own routine that feels right for you.

If you must lose weight don't starve yourself. Experiment with different programs until you find a fit. Combine that with exercise and before long you will be seeing less of you in the mirror.

> I had lost a lot of weight and I remember the pure joy of being able to cross my legs like a lady instead of a truck driver.
>
> --Immortal Alcoholic's Wife

If you are already fit, don't be complacent about your food intake. Remember you are fit because you pay attention to what you eat. Don't stop doing what you have done in the past.

I found that eating a lot of candy, cakes, chips, etc., only makes me more likely to lose my temper with my alcoholic. I'm like the baby that gets loads of sugar and then won't behave or sleep. I'm like that. Too much junk food makes me a brat. So I keep other things around to compensate for those junk food hunger pangs. I keep fruits, berries, deli meat and cheeses, and popcorn readily available just for those events.

The bottom line is to not make food the focus of your life. You have other things to do than to constantly be thinking about what's for dinner. So find what works for you and just do it. Treat food as it really is – the fuel for living your life. That's the only importance it holds.

True Confessions...
From Immortal Alcoholic blog post February 1, 2011

I succumbed to the infomercial for Jack LaLane Power Juicer. In my defense I would not even have watched the program if it had not been for Alea's telephone call telling me that we both needed one of these things. They were having a 2 for 1 special and so I took the bait and placed the order. I even upgraded to the heavy duty super duper industrial strength power unit. I bet that baby could juice a rock.

I made a special effort to buy some fresh fruits that I wouldn't normally buy – like a pineapple. Of course, when the juicer arrived I had to juice every piece of fruit in the house – oranges, apples, grapes, pineapple and then some carrots. I was a juicin' fool. I was disappointed when the fruit ran out and thought for a fleeting moment to send Riley to the store. Thank goodness I came to my senses quickly.

The best part of the experience was that everything tasted so wonderful. I usually have a glass of orange juice in the morning – you know – it comes in a half-gallon carton. But this fresh juice was so much better. I mixed the various juices together and it was such a treat. Then I added some yogurt to make a smoothie and was even more impressed.

OK. So now I'm getting all these wonderful vitamins, anti-oxidants and other healthy stuff. And I was even getting some pro-biotic from the yogurt. That lead me to thinking... hummmm... since I'm eating fresher things, maybe I should work a little harder at getting back on my diet track.

Or – maybe I could throw in a little exercise. I could take a morning walk around the paddock -- about a mile all the way around. I could work my way up to 5 miles a day. Then I thought... I might even buy a bicycle and ride around all my country roads. I work my way up and get really healthy!

Images flashed through my head of having the healthiest 62-year-old body in the county. I saw myself in size zero jeans and running marathons. I thought of tennis matches and joining the local softball team. I would be so healthy that I'd be invited to be on The Doctors!! **Oh... how glorious it was!!**

This morning I woke up and put on my sweat suit, laced up my sneakers and headed for the paddock. I opened the back door and was met with the chill from the frosty morning air. Our little red car was covered with glistening dust deposited in the middle of the night. I watched clouds of air escape from my mouth as I walked toward the fence.

I hadn't gotten far when it hit me. **Pow! I was cold!** *My hands were freezing because I forgot to wear gloves. My ears were cold because I don't have a hat or ear muffs. My knees ached from the*

*arthritis that was trying to sneak
into my joints. My nose was
running and I didn't have a tissue.*

*I headed back to the house... I
wonder how much exercise I get*

*from pushing that pusher down
into the juicer???*

CHAPTER 8

A WORD ABOUT THE FAMILY

Families come in all sizes and shapes. In my opinion most families as a whole are a bit dysfunctional. It may not be noticeable from the outside but no matter how normal a family looks there is always some little something that may seem a bit off. I have no idea what a "normal" family would look like. Growing up I thought my family was normal and in my early years, I thought my family was just like everyone else's family. As I got older, I noticed that although they may not be just like my family, they still seemed "normal" to me. So, I think that families may be different but still be normal.

It doesn't really matter whether your family is normal or dysfunctional or just plain out crazy. You don't get to choose who is in your bloodline. The good news is that families are  not always about the bloodline. Sometimes family members are people we have chosen to be in our family. I have a gigantic family but I still feel more like a sibling to some very close friends and they are the majority of my family.

Let's talk about family members who know you are the care taker of an alcoholic. If you have 20 people in your family, you will have 20 different opinions about how you should handle the situation. Some may blatantly not support you and may even end contact with you.

What do you do when someone insists their way is the way you should go? Remember that you love this person first and foremost. Remember that he/she is worried about you and only wants the best for you. It's not about being mean. It's about caring for you and not knowing really how to help. Tell that person you love him/her and appreciate that they care about you. Don't give that person a string of reasons why you can't do as they insist. It will be perceived as excuses rather than viable reasons. If it comes down to a hostile situation or the person saying they will cut you out of his/her life if you don't comply. Tell them you will miss the person and let go.

You might be surprised as you discover who will support you even if they disagree and who will walk away. Just know that these people may leave you for awhile, but eventually they will be back. It will hurt. But don't dwell on those feelings. You need positivity and positive people. Kick the negative out the front door.

Make sure that the people who are supportive and understanding know that you appreciate them and show your gratitude in any way you can. It will pay you back in the end. In order to take care of yourself you must take care of those who support you.

My point is the individuals that compose a family all have individual personalities and will have their own opinions. They will most likely express those opinions. It's OK. Just because they express them doesn't mean you have to follow through on each person's advice. Don't forget you are an individual as well and have your own opinions and a right to act on them.

My Uncle Hank
From Immortal Alcoholic blog December 20, 2012

Growing up in a very large family created special holiday experiences. I always thought that would be the way Christmas would be every year for the rest of my life. What we think when we are growing up doesn't always turn out to be the reality when we reach adulthood and seems to fall farther from reality as we reach our senior years.

I didn't grow up in an alcoholic home. I can only remember one family member that may have had alcohol issues. Uncle Hank was the husband of my father's sister — so my aunt's husband. He was a handsome guy with dark wavy hair and blue eyes. He had a wiry build and rumor had it that he had been so injured during World War II that most of his body was held together with wire and screws. He seemed to be in pain most of the time, but was never daunted by physical labor. He fit in well with the other hard-working family members.

My aunt was head over heels in love with Uncle Hank. You could see it in her eyes. Everyone knew that nothing would ever come between them. But, he had a darker side to him as well. He was a firm believer that sparing the rod, boot, belt or fist would definitely spoil the child. He would demand silence and when his demand was not met; his children would cower in fear. Even so, his wife and kids were the world to him.

I cannot talk about the dark stuff without mentioning that he was also a very funny fellow. He could always tell a good joke and get everyone laughing. He knew when to keep it clean for the kids and a bit raunchy for the adults. Things were always light-hearted when their family came to visit ours. Christmas visits were always extra special.

One year my aunt wanted Santa to bring her a Hammond Organ. It was all she wanted, but she believed that it was not within their budget, so she never pushed Uncle Hank to deliver. That was the year that all the families converged upon my parent's house to celebrate Christmas together. All total there were 23 kids in the house under the age of 18. My mother cleared out the office and one of the bedrooms and turned the rooms into a wall-to-wall mattress where the kids could fall asleep at will.

It was getting late and those of us who were not asleep were talking softly so as not to wake the other kids. The laundry room was just on the other side of the door. We could hear bits and pieces of conversation from the kitchen where the adults were gathered around the table telling stories of the past and happily cajoling each other. Uncle Hank was in the laundry room. He was crumpling up paper every few minutes he would let out a howl of laughter but said nothing. Occasionally, he would ask my mother to fix him another high-ball and bring it to him. My mother did as he asked. We counted how many times the request was made and granted – nine times. Nine high-balls in the space of two hours which really meant nothing to us children because what did we know after all?

Christmas morning we woke up to find Santa had, in fact, found his way to our house. We had to step over presents to get to our individual treasures. We were in Christmas heaven. Kathy went to Uncle Hank and gave him a big hug. His hands were shaking and he had an awful smell to him. His wife came into the room with a shot of whiskey and a cup of hot black coffee. He seemed to be in a much better mood after downing the little glass of golden liquid.

When it came time for the gifts to be handed out, the fathers each took turns pulling a gift out from under the tree and handing it over to the designated recipient. The system continued until there was only one box left. It was a box the size of a refrigerator and was wrapped in a patchwork of bits and pieces of left-over holiday paper. The box was to my aunt from Uncle Hank. This was the box that had provided so much laughter from him in the laundry room the night before.

My aunt started out by being careful, but that idea quickly fell by the wayside. She tore open the box and it was filled with newspaper. She looked at Uncle Hank and he told her to keep searching. Taped to the very bottom of the box was a Christmas card with a note that said her Hammond Organ would be delivered when they returned to their home. She hugged him and planted a sloppy romantic kiss on his lips. The kids giggled and laughed. My aunt cried. And the best part of Christmas morning was over.

There was breakfast and then food flowed freely from the kitchen for the entire rest of the day. We always had a sit-down Christmas dinner and that was no different this year. The whiskey also flowed into my uncle's glass continuously. I had never noticed anyone's drinking habits before, but that year I was acutely aware of how many times Uncle Hank refilled his glass. I lost track because it seemed his glass was never empty.

For me and the other kids, it wasn't a big deal. Uncle Hank was happy and there was no strict punishment dealt during their visit. There were no angry arguments – as sometimes happen when the entire family convenes. It was just a good day creating good memories.

Uncle Hank died just a few years later. They lived in the mountains and his commute to town was over the winding highway. He missed a turn and his van ran over a cliff. My aunt and the two children were devastated. We were all told that he had fallen asleep and that's what caused him to miss the curve in the road.

As an adult, I once asked my mother if Uncle Hank had been driving drunk. She responded "Why NO! Why would you think such a thing?" I said I was just wondering because he was such a good driver. I never told her that I remembered him drinking constantly during that Christmas holiday. After all, I was just a child. Maybe I remembered it all wrong. But, I don't think so.

CHAPTER 9

FINANCIAL HEALTH

> *Money isn't the most important thing in life, but it's reasonably close to oxygen on the 'gotta have it' scale.*
>
> --Zig Ziglar

I didn't learn much about money when I was growing up. The one thing that I did know as a fact was that there was never enough of it. I really don't know how my parents did it with ten mouths around the dinner table and five kids needing the necessities of life. My Mom stayed at home while we were young and my Dad was the only bread winner. But they managed and I wish they had taught me some of their tricks.

If you believe that your finances have nothing to do with surviving alcoholic chaos, please reconsider that thought. There is nothing more depressing than putting up with an alcoholic who always finds the cash for a bottle when there is no milk in the fridge. It's stressful and stress is not good for you either physically or mentally.

I'm just going to give you a few tips/suggestions that I have learned from the school of stupid actions. Hopefully, you won't learn the same way I did. Some of this information will seem redundant and that I'm just telling you the obvious. I know. That's what I thought too until I actually started putting some of those cliché's to work for me.

Have a budget

Having a budget doesn't mean you scribble a few things on a piece of paper and call it a budget. I use an Excel spreadsheet, but you can do it by hand on a columned piece of paper.

On the left hand side write down all your expenses that you are required to pay each and every month. Put the necessities (rent, utilities, savings, etc) as a group; monthly payments (credit cards, gym membership, etc.); insurance payments (life, health, etc.); car expenses (payments, insurance, upkeep) home maintenance expenses (yard service, repair costs, etc.); food; and any other expenses (clothing, etc.) you encounter in a month's time. You can also make a group for entertaining and things you want to save enough money to be able to make the expenditure.

You are going to use this budget sheet to not only remind you of what you must pay and how much, but also to record any expenditure that you make during that month. If you hadn't planned on buying a coat, but there was this big sale… you need to list it on your budget sheet.

Near bottom of the sheet add your totals for what you spent during the month. Then list your income sources and the average amount you can expect to receive. (I list my social security income as a constant never changing amount.) When you receive money from an unexpected source – like winning the lottery – make sure you list it on your budget sheet.

Subtract your expenses from your income and if you are lucky you will come out on the positive side Often you will be in the negative. That's when you have to go back into your budget and make some adjustments. There are payments that never change like your rent and car payments. But others can be reduced like your food costs. You will have to manipulate things around until you are in the black.

The current month budget sheet is what I use on almost a daily basis as I adjust, readjust, make payments, spend money, etc. As payments are made, I highlight the amount so I know it's been paid. At the end of the month I should be able to see what I paid and exactly where my money went.

After three months you will have a good average of your monthly expenses. Use those figures to budget into your future.

Budget Worksheet (Monthly)

Below is a sample of my budget worksheet:

Paydate for Month of __October__	1st	5th	25th	Total
ACTUAL EXPENDITURES				
Rent / Mortgage	$1,500			$1,500
Electricity		$300		$300
Car Payment			$250	$250
Food	$150	$150	$150	$450
Household Supplies	$100	$50	$25	$175
Savings	$100	$100	$100	$300
Total Amount Paid for Expenses	$1,850	$600	$525	$2,975
Income	$2,400	$1,200	$1,200	$4,800
Balance (Income minus Amount Paid)	$550	$600	$675	$1,825

Make two worksheets for each month. Use one as your **projected expenses** and the other as the **actual expenses.** As the year progresses transfer your figures to a **yearly worksheet.** At the start of the New Year you can use the previous year's figures to predict the next years expenses. This will make planning your financial future a bit easier. You will also be able to see where you are spending too much or too little.

I use an Excel spreadsheet but you can also use a columnar tablet that you can buy from your office supply store.

Annual Expense Tracking Worksheet

Below is a sample of my annual expense tracking worksheet

Year 2016	Jan	Feb	Mar	Apr
Rent / Mortgage	$1,500	$1,500	$1,500	$1,500
Electricity	$300	$300	$250	$325
Car Payment	$250	$250	$250	$250
Food	$450	$450	$500	$525
Household Supplies	$175	$200	$100	$225
Savings	$300	$300	$300	$300
Total Amount Paid for Expenses	$2,975	$3,000	$2,900	$3,250
Income	$4,800	$4,800	$4,800	$4,800
Balance (Income minus Amount Paid)	$1,825	$1800	$1,900	$1,550

Savings

The ideal thing to do is take your savings right off the top of income. Put the money somewhere – a bank savings account, in your piggy bank, behind a picture on your wall, or anyplace else that will keep it separate from all your other expenses.

It doesn't have to be much. As little as $10 a month will still work but the more you deposit the faster it will grow. Don't think about it. Just do it and forget about it. Saying to yourself that you'll just take the money out of your savings if you hit a snag in the budget is just NOT acceptable. This is true "rainy day" money or your "get away" fund.

Don't tell anyone you have it. Especially don't tell the alcoholic because he will be searching the house so he can use it to buy booze.

Taxes

Get a good tax account to help you with your taxes. I use:

Gina Mewes
386-747-9097
112 W. Indiana Ave, Suite 205
Deland, FL 32720
gina@ginamewes.com.

If you are behind on your taxes, get them caught up now. They are not going to go away and the IRS WILL make you miserable until they have every penny they say you owe them.

Gina has been a lifesaver for me by helping me put my IRS woes behind me. I'm not worried about my bank account being emptied or my check being garnished.

If you don't want to use Gina, find another tax accountant that can help you get back to sleeping at need. It will relieve a lot of stress from your existence.

Prepare for the worst

Make a plan for what you are going to do if either you or the alcoholic die or become to ill to take care of yourself. Meet with an estate lawyer for advice.

Plan out your funeral like it's just another event. You don't have to follow through on it because you just want to know the cost of what you would want. Do the same thing for the alcoholic.

Once you have a firm idea of what it will cost you decide on how you will pay for it. Do you have a life insurance policy? Or a long-term care policy? Maybe you need to start setting aside a few dollars a month to help you when the time comes. Put it as an expense on your budget sheet. DO NOT combine this expense with your savings expense.

In conclusion

If you are in a negative place with your money, find a way to resolve it. Maybe you have some assets you could sell? Or maybe you should consider moving to less costly housing? Refinance your house and/or car to get a smaller payment. Downsize and have a yard sale.

You may decide to go back to work. If you haven't worked in a while consider going to a temporary employment agency. By taking temp jobs you can sort of "test the water" before committing to any particular job. The downside is that going to work may mean that you must employ help in taking care of the alcoholic in the home. You don't want to spend your new found wages by paying it all to the new caregiver. However, somethings getting out of the house is worth the price of a baby-sitter.

The point of this chapter is to help take some stress away from your everyday life. In the next few chapters you will need all the energy can must to save yourself. Surviving is hard work.

Financial Pit of Despair
From Immoratal Alcoholic blog post June 1, 2015

During the days when Riley was drinking and we were together, often times more money would be spent on booze than the total amount of our utility bills. I tried everything I knew to make sure I got the paycheck before he had a chance to cash it. Because once it was cashed, it was basically gone. (That was before the days of direct deposit.) When he ran out of cash, he would write a check. I ended up closing the bank accounts to prevent paying return check fees.

Riley earned enough money to support our family. But, I worked two, sometimes three, jobs in order to keep food on the table. I don't think he even knew how much money he was spending. He didn't have to because I managed the money. Trusting him with the task was not something I was comfortable with.

During the times when Riley was sober, we would sit down every Sunday and do the budget. He didn't seem concerned that there was always something that didn't get paid. We always paid our basic living expenses first, then we bought groceries and after that everything just got rotated around. If we paid on bill A this month, we would pay bill B next month we never got through all the letters in the alphabet when he would start drinking again.

If you are in the rare position of being financially solvent in spite of the alcoholic's spending, I would suggest that you prepare now for a possible decline. How many times have you heard, "A penny saved is a penny earned." Or "You should always save for a rainy day." Those statements are never truer than for someone involved with an alcoholic. If you live today as though you are already in financial trouble, maybe trouble won't knock on your door.

Here are some things you might consider doing:

Make a monthly spreadsheet budget and for the next six months enter the estimated amount of payments and in the next column, enter the actual amount spent. After six months you will see if your estimations are close to the actual average amount spent. Now you know how much you should be entering in the estimation column. I keep my spreadsheet open on my desktop. That way if I need to spend money, I can easily check to see if I can afford the expense.

Pay yourself first. I don't care if you use a piggy bank, a lock box, or a secret savings account. Put a little aside in case of an emergency or if you are planning a "get away." An emergency is NOT about keeping the alcoholic in booze. This money is to be used if the lights get turned off or if you decide to leave. But never use this money to support his addiction.

Learn to clip coupons and find out

what stores double up. You don't have to be an extreme couponer – just a wise shopper. It takes a bit of time to develop a couponing routine, but it's worth it in the end. Motivate yourself by putting the "amount saved" in your emergency cash stash.

Buy clothing "off season". You can shop for clothing and put them away until the time is right for wearing them. It's not just clothes. Lawn supplies can be bought in the fall and saved until next spring. Watch the clearance sections wherever you shop. Go there first and see what they have that you can use.

If you are trying to climb out of the hole of despair, call the creditors or collection agents and try to negotiate some kind of repayment plan. Pay yourself first – as above. That's more important than ever if you're struggling. Consider bankruptcy. Get advice from people or places like your bank or a social service agency that offers financial counseling. Sometimes you can find a professional financial advisor to help for a reasonable fee. That advisor can help you decide if it is time to file bankruptcy or give you suggestions on how to get back on track.

My cousin recommended an advisor named Gina Mewes. She helped me clear up all my back taxes and removed the garnishments from our paychecks. I had thought that we would have to file bankruptcy, but as it turns out, with the tax issue gone, I can negotiate with all the other creditors and avoid bankruptcy. It has been a welcomed relief. She gave me advice on getting a business license and whether or not we should file joint or separate returns. I discovered that I didn't know as much as I thought I did – that's what happens when you think you know it ALL. With the garnishments gone, I could easily afford her rates.

Gina has offered to give special consideration to any of my blog readers who find themselves in trouble with the IRS. Her contact information is on her website http://www.taxandbusinessmanagement.com/. Be sure to let her know that read about her on Linda's blog.

My point is, plan for a financial disaster even if you are not in one now. If you're already in a financial pit, keep working towards climbing out. Seek advice and plan for the next disaster now, before the storm hits

I believe the topic of money is very important and anyone involved with an alcoholic should be aware of consequences that happen. Below is an example of what can happen to a totally unexpecting couple who would never dream of being in their situation.

Drunk Driving Bitch
From Immortal Alcoholic blog dated December 29, 2011

As we approach the New Years Eve party extravaganza, I feel that driving need to talk about drunk driving – again.

I live in a "community property" state. That means whatever is his is hers and vice versa. If a divorce takes place the property can be slip right down the middle. Assets, such as houses and cars, are sold for the cash and then the cash is divided 50%-50%. The same thing goes for the bills. All the money is added up and each much pay half of the bill to close out the account. Of course, what most likely happens is that the couple comes to some kind of amicable agreement about who actually gets or pays for what. At least, that's what normally happens if one part of the couple isn't driven by greed or insanity.

Let's do a hypothetical:

You've been married to your spouse, Jane, for 25 years and have never entertained the thought of getting a divorce. She's a good wife, excellent mother and fabulous lover who understands you totally and completely. **Boy – those marriages are rare – aren't you a lucky guy!!**

Jane works for a travel agency and she has just closed a deal that sold out the entire cruise ship for a famous cruise line. The revenue earned is in six figures. The whole office is elated and everyone wants to celebrate the good fortune. She calls you and says she will not be able to get home for dinner, but she's ordered take-out to be delivered so you won't have to worry. **Wow! She thought about your needs and accommodated for not being able to fix dinner. She's the best!**

The entire office group piles in their individual cars and heads up the road to a four-star steakhouse and karaoke bar. A couple of Appletini's get things loosened up and when dinner arrives, a couple of bottles of champagne are uncorked. Talk is flowing freely, passes are made, and how about a bottle of wine to go with the prime rib? Oh – there are so many of us – we need a couple bottles. Someone is having chicken, so that's a bottle of white. A glass of brandy with dessert and then everyone heads to the bar for some nails-on-the-chalkboard singing of "You Light Up My Life".

Jane deserves to have a good time and she's partaking in it all, the appltini's, champagne, wine, brandy and a couple drinks to get up enough courage to go on stage. She knows she's probably had too much to drink, so she starts *ordering coffee. The steakhouse is not in the best neighborhood and she doesn't want to leave her brand new Aviator in the parking lot. She thinks if she just sits and drinks coffee for a while she'll be fine to drive home and thereby avoid leaving her car and taking a taxi.*

Just before Jane leaves the bar, she calls you to tell you she's on her way home. You tell her, NO. Wait there, you'll come get her. But she insists she's OK to drive and for you not to worry. She sounded fine, so you give in to her wishes.

An hour later, and after much flirting with the Daniel Craig-ish bartender, Jane gets into her Aviator and drives a few blocks when it happens. Jane runs a red light and slams into the driver side of a car from the cross street. She is not injured and runs from the car to help the driver from the other car. There is blood everywhere and the driver is moaning in pain. Jane calls 911 who responds quickly to her call.

Jane is arrested and taken to jail for drunk driving. The injured driver dies on the way to the hospital while Jane, in her neat little three-piece suit, primly waits inside a cell, for you to bail her out. She is stoic and remorseful that she has caused so much damage from her night of libations. But, she has never been in trouble before and isn't sure what exactly to expect.

Fast-forward to months down the road, Jane has been to court, fined, put on probation and is moving on with her life. You've discovered that Jane was having an affair with the bartender at the steakhouse and you've filed for divorce. You are also moving on with your life. You have custody of the kids and your family home. You've just taken a very well-paying job and look forward to vacations with the kids on the beaches of Cabo San Lucas.

But wait --- the family of the injured driver has filed a suit against Jane and her "estate" for damages resulting from the death of the driver. You think this is a hard blow for Jane, but it really has nothing to do with you even though you are also named in the suit. Jane has next to nothing in her estate to give the family of the dead driver and the two of you go to court.

The judge sits up on his high bench and you can't believe what you are hearing. You live in a community property state and the "estate" includes everything you both own jointly and separately while you were married. The accident happened before a divorce was obtained, so you are also liable for the expenses incurred as well as Jane. The court orders a judgment in the amount of millions and you sit in amazement as you realize that you and Jane, together, must come up with this money. Your life will never, ever, be the same. Financially, you are destroyed.

Jane, your wonderfully loving and

considerate wife, turned drunken adulteress, has taken your idyllic life from you and **you** *must* PAY *for it.* **Life truly sucks.**

Back to reality –

This is New Year's Eve coming up here – like soon. Maybe it's time to start planning on protecting yourself for the possible outfall of a night of celebrating the forthcoming fresh New Year. I'm well aware that I'm suggesting that you do what is nearly impossible to achieve. I'm suggesting that you find a way to keep the alcoholic in your life from getting behind that wheel and ruining the lives of many people – your life included.

I'm fortunate that I don't have to worry about Riley driving. I'm a bitch about the whole car issue. I refuse to get his car registered or make it drivable. But, if he did have access to a car, I would probably be enough of a bitch to keep it from moving out of my driveway. One of the tires would mysteriously go flat, or the keys would be missing, or maybe I'd remove a couple of fuses.

I once read where a woman made one of those magnetic signs and put it on the back of her husband's car -- just above the license plate. It read – **"I'm a drunk driver. Please call 911 and stop me from killing someone."** *It was in big letters and very noticeable if you just happened to be sitting at a light behind this car. Her husband drove an SUV and he never thought to look at the back of the car before leaving the house.*

When the husband got out of jail, he reveled in telling all his friends about what a bitch his wife was to put that sign there and cause him to get arrested.

Her response – "I am proud to be a bitch and we are both lucky that you've taught me how to be one."

CHAPTER 10

ACCEPTANCE

In spite of what some people may say you are not crazy. It can be perceived as being crazy to take care of an alcoholic. After all who in their right mind would do that under any circumstances. Well, you are doing it whether you volunteered or not, it is an issue you must deal with now. Learn to accept your situation and make the most of it. I am not here to judge you and neither should anyone else be judging you..

Al-Anon has a list of steps that will aide you in your journey for sanity. I'm not 100% on board with all the Al-Anon teachings, but they are a good place to start when looking for others who share your plight. If you don't like what you learn there, simply let it go. If you don't feel comfortable, don't go back. You have the freedom to choose what you wish to do.

> *Sometimes your heart needs more time to accept what your mind already knows.*
> --Author Unknown

There is an issue on which Al-Anon and I both agree. And that is on the subject of "acceptance". In order to survive you must accept a few things as the way they are. If you try to change these things, you are not ready to do what is necessary to survive.

If things DO change, it isn't because you have manipulated some magic formula. It will simply be a side-effect of working on yourself and not the alcoholic. If a chance for the better does materialize, it's a side-effect of all the work you have been doing on yourself. Accept the change and enjoy it while you have it.

Below are the things you must learn to accept as facts.

Your alcoholic is not going to stop drinking.

Alcoholics drink because that's what they do. To expect them not to drink is setting yourself up for disappointment. They may have periods of abstinence, but they most likely will eventually go back to the bottle. Some

manage to stay sober, but those who do must focus entirely on their sobriety which means the loved ones are still low on the priority level.

You are not responsible for his alcoholism

There's always an excuse when the alcoholic starts to explain why they keep drinking. Usually they blame everyone and everything on why they downed a liter of booze No one understands them. The spouse or children are their problem. On the job, the alcoholic perceives an atmosphere of disapproval. Even the mailman is at fault because he has not received notification of winning Publisher's Clearing House.

The only one responsible for the alcoholic's addiction to alcohol is the alcoholic. That is the only person who can decide to over-indulge with a liquid that is toxic to the body.

You cannot cure the alcoholic

So if you are not responsible for the alcoholism, maybe you can help with reaching sobriety. Right? Wrong. You are the last person who might be able to help him with his disease. It's not your disease, not your responsibility, and, definitely, not yours to "fix."

The only cure for alcoholism is to stop drinking. You have no control over that happening. If you have taken the first step to heart, then you already accept that he is not going to stop drinking. Now you must accept that you cannot cure him of this awful disease.

Your goals do not match the alcoholic's.

If you are the spouse of the alcoholic you probably remember talking about your future as a couple. You made plans and discussed what your life would look like in 25, 50, or more years. You knew what you wanted and vowed to work hard as a unit to make your dreams become a reality.

Once the alcoholic takes over, any goals or dreams cease to exist. The reality sets in that the only goal the alcoholic has to be able to end the day in a drunken stupor.

You have not changed. You still want that house with the little white picket fence or four kids and two dogs or the corner office in a large corporation business. You still have your goals intact. The only difference is that you are now alone in making your dreams come true.

The alcoholic is walking a different path and will not provide much support as you struggle to fulfill your goals.

No amount of love will make it any better.

If all we needed was love to make a perfect world, we would have no hungry children, no wars and world peace. There are just some things love can't fix and one of those things is drug and alcohol abuse. It's impossible to "love" the disease out of the alcoholic.

You were born into this world as an individual.

We arrive into this world as one person – even if you are a twin or triple. You are an individual unto yourself. You are unique and are priceless. Your life is a blank slate and what you do with it is entirely up to you.

You have the ability to make your own decisions.

The right to make decisions about what/where/when/why you do things is completely yours. Sometimes it might take some research and polling of those your trust, but in the end you are the one who says yes or not to anything in your life.

The alcoholic will try to convince you that you don't know your own mind. That's so he/she can maintain control of your actions around the drinking.

Don't let the alcoholic take away your power. Decide for yourself what you want and how to go about getting it. Then take action on whatever decision you have made.

Being happy is your decision and only yours.

You must decide to be happy. Once you have made and committed to being happy, the bad things won't seem so bad anymore.

Things around you may be falling apart but you can hold on to your happiness. It doesn't mean that you will not feel sadness or despair because you certainly will. But you will not lose yourself in those negative emotions.

Deciding to be happy means whatever the alcoholic is doing or chaos being created, is something you can stand back from and watch rather than participate. Yes, you may have to something to protect yourself. But it is just that – doing something and not taking it all on as if you created the mess in the first place.

A State of Mind…
From Immortal Alcoholic blog dated May 10, 2015

I've been spending a lot of time with my cousins lately. Over the past 20 years we haven't had much contact. They are older than me and I think it was only natural that we distanced ourselves unintentionally. We became the relatives that we saw at weddings and funerals. Of course, we always said we'd stay in touch, but that seldom happened.

This reconnection began when one cousin called and said they would like to visit for a few days. I was so excited I coulda pee'd me pants. We had a wonderful visit and while he was here, he put me in touch with his sister. AWESOME!

In one of our conversations the sister asked me "Are you happy?"

if after everything I've been, and am still, going through, could I still say I was happy in my life. I had to think about it for a minute or two.

Wikipedia defines happiness as: "Happiness is a mental or emotional state of well-being defined by positive or pleasant emotions ranging from contentment to intense joy."

I believe we all have the capacity to be happy even though we may feel sad, unsettled, disappointed, unloved, unappreciated or discontented. All of those feelings define each of us at various periods in our lives. But they don't have to define our entire life.

I'm reminded of a time when a teenage boyfriend moved away and I knew in my heart I would never see him again. I was devastated, inconsolable, and knew I would just never be happy again. But shortly thereafter, I met a new potential boyfriend and the sun shone brightly upon me once again. Between the boyfriends, I grew to accept that Boyfriend A was in my past and that life was really not that bad. I started smiling and laughing and slowly I returned to a state of happiness. Once I reached the happiness state I was open to meeting Boyfriend B.

My point is that we go through things that are horribly painful at any moment in time. Sometimes those moments last for years, like the death of my son. It's OK to feel that sadness, pain or whatever emotion that's going on, but even inside that painful bubble, we can step aside and have moments of happiness. The more often we have the happy moments, the more we will want them and reach for them until they become a way of life once again. The sadness doesn't go away, it just gets pushed aside.

In my current world, I pushed my former happily single life aside to become the caregiver of my estranged husband. Did my decision make me happy? Of course not, there wasn't any joy in taking care of a narcissistic, controlling, drunk while he is potty-ing in his pants, and being otherwise obnoxious. But it was a decision I made and had to learn how to prevent him from destroying my happiness. I had to learn to be happy in spite of the decision. And that's what I did.

I compartmentalized my emotions concerning my husband and made sure I developed my own interests that created a sense of accomplishment, satisfaction and/or contentedness. As I continued doing the things outside of my husband's needs/wants, my happiness factor became larger and more clearly defined. I wasn't happy about caregiving my husband, but I was happy with the fact that it lead me to being happy in a different way. From the unhappiness, I became happy.

To answer my cousin's question – YES. I am generally happy. I have a happy life that is often filled with emotional strife and stress.

Would I change anything in the past? – Probably. But, I can use the past to help me cope or create my future.

She asks how I got to be in a happy place? I told her I made a choice to be happy. If I had made any other choice, it would mean that grief, disillusionment, disappointment, anger, and a host of other emotions would win the constant battle that goes on inside everyone's psyche. If I take down my shield and just let them all run roughshod over me, they win. Every bad thing that has ever happened to me wins and all the good is destroyed. I keep my "happiness army" strong by practicing happiness every day. It's like an exercise. Even when I don't really feel happy, I find something to be happy about and make that the focus of my day. The more I express happiness, the more I feel happiness.

This morning I was rudely awakened by my dog barking at the deer grazing in my back yard. I was irritated because it was only 4:00 a.m. I got up, made the coffee and grumbled about wishing I could sleep in on this Sunday. With my coffee in hand, I looked out the patio door and saw the MaMa and Baby deer. I'm happy I have a yard the deer like to visit. I'm happy my dog woke me up so I could enjoy watching them. I'm happy that waking up early gave me time to write this post.

I am a happy woman.

CHAPTER 11

DISCOVER YOURSELF

Who You Are

If someone asked who you are, what would your answer be? I think that is one of the hardest questions for me to answer. There are all sorts of adjectives to describe who I am, but that doesn't really tell the WHO of who I am.

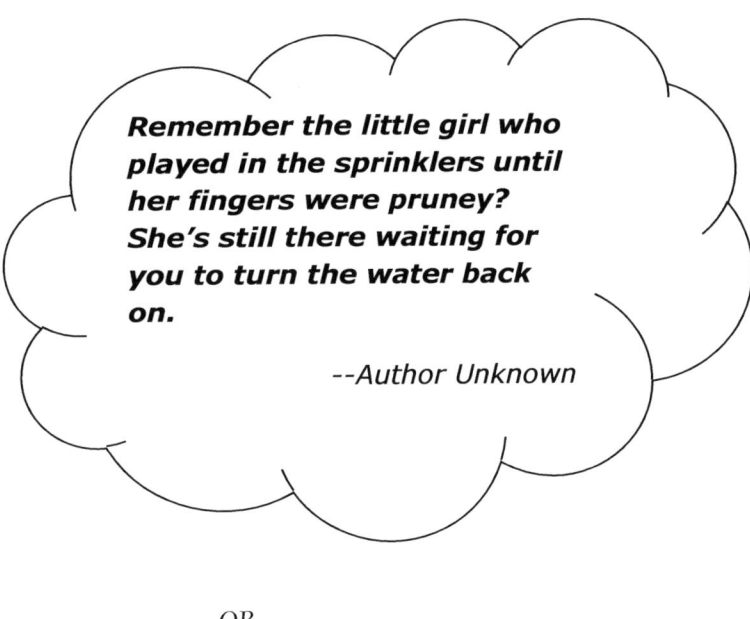

I'm Linda, a family oriented woman of strength, determination and creativity. I am an author and advocate to caregivers of alcoholics. Being a grandmother and great-grandmother is the best part of my life.

OR

I'm Linda, the Immortal Alcoholic's Wife, caregiver, grandmother, of strong work ethic. I'm an author, crafter, seamstress and retired real estate title examiner.

OR

My name is Linda. I'm a great-grandmother who encourages and supports all of my children both blood and heart. I am an author who is sensitive to the needs and circumstances of caregivers to alcoholics. I'm a child of the 50s and am nostalgic for the time and place of my childhood. I'm an optimistic realist who meets life with a positive attitude.

Which of the descriptions helps you to know about who I really am? Actually, all of them describe a portion of who and what I'm about. I would use some kind of version of these depending on the group dynamics and the situation.

Write down several versions of who you are. (There's a form for this exercise at the end of this section.) When you finish look at them and think about whether it is an accurate description of you. It's best to put them aside and come back to them at a later time. That way you can see them with a fresh perspective. Make adjustments if you feel they are necessary.

Now that you know who you are, what are you about? What are your interests, hobbies, enjoyments? My list would read something like:

I love to write books, blogs, stories mostly non-fiction;

I enjoy doing home crafts like making wreaths and decorations;

I'm a seamstress and enjoy sewing for children more than adults;

I like to cook but only when I am in a large, well-equipped kitchen using both old and new recipes.

From that list of items combined with the introductory statements, you should have a pretty good idea of who I am and what I'm about.

Write your own list of what you are about using the things you like most in life.

Now put your introductory statement with the list following it. This is **Who You Are** and **What You Are About**. You are <u>not</u> Linda, Riley's wife, Lois's daughter, etc. **You are You** and that's something unique to anyone else.

Who is _____ (your name)?

Description of who you are: (This is a rough draft. You'll do a finalized statement at the end of the exercise.)	
Version 1:	
Version 2:	
Version 3:	

What you are about

List items in the order in which they are important in your life. For example, if a hobby is the most liked thing for you, list the hobby and place the number 1 in the Order column. Then if the next is an Interest, list it next and put a 2 in the Order column. You can list everything you want and place the Order numbers at the end if that is easier.

Order	Interests	Hobbies	Causes	Entertainment	Other

Occupation:

Current			
Previous			
Trained			
When I grow up			
Dream Job			

Fill in the blanks of this statement: (Use the forms on the previous pages to determine the answers.)

My name is	
	Name
I am a/an	
	Trait, occupation, etc
A little extra something	
	You may not know this about me
I aspire to	
	Goals, dreams, plans, hopes

NOW WRITE YOUR STATEMENT TELLING WHO YOU ARE:

Making Time

Now that you have this new information, how much time do you spend on doing the things on your list? For several days (a week is great) keep track of what you do. If you attend to the alcoholic, write it down as a task that you perform daily or weekly or however often. After the week ends you should be able to see how much time you spend on each of your tasks.

How much time do you spend on any of the things in your **What You Are About** List? My time sheet would look like this:

	Mid	1	2	3	4	5	6	7	8	9	10	11	N	1	2	3	4	5	6	7	8	9	10	11
TASK	Prepare breakfast for Riley																						
TASK	Straightening Riley's room / prep for day																						
TASK	Writing new book																						
TASK	Prepare lunch for Riley and dinner																						
TASK	Change Rile's underwear																						
TASK	Get snacks/water/soda for Riley																						
TASK	Watch soaps																						
TASK	General Housekeeping, Budgeting, Etc.																						
TASK	Do craft item																						
TASK	Monitor FB, Blog, Websites (multi-tasked)																						
TASK	Watch Evening TV																						

Task	Total Time Spent	Enjoyment Level
Caregiving Riley	10 hours	3
General Household Upkeep	6 hours	5
Time doing my own thing	25 hours	9
Total number of Tasks __3__ Totals	41	17

Results:
On a scale of 1 to 10, how much did you enjoy this day? _5.5_
Add the numbers in the Enjoyment column and divide by the number of tasks and that's your Enjoyment Level.

How much time did you spent enjoying your day? _25 out of 41_
Add up the time you spent doing the tasks that you most enjoyed.

Fortunately, I seem to be giving more time to myself rather than Riley and the household stuff. The large number is accountable to multi-tasking which is OK, but feels a bit deceptive. If I discount the monitoring of the websites, then I need to subtract 14 hours from my 25 hours leaving me with giving 11 hours to myself. In that case I'm spending 16 hours a day on Riley and housekeeping and 11 for me. That's not too bad but I'd like to tip the scales in the other direction.

If you are not giving any time to yourself, it's time to make a change. You must have time during the day to do the things you WANT to do and not just the things you HAVE to do.

Make a plan for your day and before you schedule anything put in some time for what you want to do. Then adjust the other available time around your preferred activity.

I know that for most of us, a day is never the same and can seldom be planned out exactly. This is where multi-tasking can be a lifesaver. I do craft projects while watching afternoon soaps. I bake while cooking dinner. In between tasks I'm often at the computer.

The point is that you can't be YOU if you are not actively being YOU. If you are only doing for the alcoholic, you are simply being who he needs you to be. If you want to survive the chaos that the alcoholic creates, you must have a life worthy of your survival. Otherwise you will simply fade away and possibly die long before the alcoholic.

On the next page you will find some worksheets that will help you see where your time is going and how much of it is spent on caregiving and how much is spent on things you enjoy doing. The goal is to achieve a balance of things you don't like versus the things that you like. The ultimate goal is to tip the balance in favor of the things that make you who you want to be rather than focusing all you time on the alcoholic.

Being YOU means making the time to be YOU.

Current and Daily Time Sheets

Use a color pencil (you can use a different color for each task to make things more interesting) and shade in the blocks when you are doing the listed task. You can overlap the time blocks for different tasks. For example, you may be doing laundry while you are cooking dinner.

	Mid	1	2	3	4	5	6	7	8	9	10	11	N	1	2	3	4	5	6	7	8	9	10	11
							AM												PM					
TASK																								
TASK																								
TASK																								
TASK																								
TASK																								
TASK																								
TASK																								
TASK																								
TASK																								
TASK																								
TASK																								
TASK																								
TASK																								
TASK																								
TASK																								

Current and Daily Actual Total Time:

Enter the tasks completed or whatever you did, the amount of time it took you to do the task and rate how much you enjoyed the task on a scale of 1-10 with 10 meaning you loved, loved, loved it and 1 being that you hated it more than having every bone in your body broken.

Task	Total Time Spent	Enjoyment Level
Total number of Tasks _____ Totals		

Results:

On a scale of 1 to 10, how much did you enjoy this day? _____
Add the numbers in the Enjoyment column and divide by the number of tasks and that's your Enjoyment Level.

How much time did you spent enjoying your day? _____
Add up the time you spent doing the tasks that you most enjoyed.

Personality Tests

Just for fun you might want to try taking some personality tests and see how close the tests come to what you believe is your personality. If you take five or more tests, you can compare them to determine which tests agree. The more tests that come up with similar results, the more likely you have that trait.

Reminder – these tests are really just a form of entertainment and are not meant to be set in store descriptions of your personality.

Here's where to find some of the on-line tests:

http://personality-testing.info/ -- As per the site, "This website provides a collection of interactive personality tests with detailed results that can be taken for personal entertainment or to learn more about personality assessment. These tests range from very serious and widely used scientific instruments popular psychology to self-produced quizzes. A special focus is given to the strengths, weaknesses and validity of the various systems."

https://www.themuse.com/advice/14-free-personality-tests-thatll-help-you-figure-yourself-out -- As per the site, "To Find Out Your Overall Personality Type. If you want to go the super broad route, these are the best options to tackle every aspect of who you are in one shot.

Have fun!

He's the sick one – not me
From Immortal Alcoholic blog January 12, 2012

I believe that anyone who is in an emotional arm's distance from any alcoholic/addict needs to find recovery just as much as the one who has the focus of our attention. That's just it right there – the one who has the focus of our attention. What about turning some of that attention on you -- the caregiver?

As we get drawn into this world of "keeping things going" we often lose sight of our own needs and happiness. We must put ourselves at a lower priority level because we have no idea what is going to happen next in our homes as a result of the alcoholic's brain damaged stupidity. We are always on alert. We must pay attention to them – the alcoholic, kids, parents, siblings, neighbors, friends, co-workers – we must be aware of what they are doing, thinking, seeing. I'm tired just thinking about it all.

Detachment is the best way to survive life in an alcoholic home. It sounds like a dirty word, but all it really means is to take care of your own self. As long as you are constantly worrying about what the alcoholic is doing to everyone else and to himself, you might forget to so things that make you happy.

And – what DOES make you happy?? Do you even know what makes you happy? Have you forgotten what makes you smile? I preach all the time (to anyone who will listen) to find your passion. Find that one thing that you love doing and then do it.

I know what you are thinking "I love to do "X", but I just don't have the time or the money." If it is truly your passion you will find a way to be involved somehow. Love to read – volunteer at the local library. Love animals – volunteer at the animal shelter. Love to cook – volunteer at your local soup kitchen. There are lots of ways to do things you love that won't cost you anything and just might help someone else in the process.

If you have the funds available and you like doing things like, horseback riding, spa days, etc, then set aside one day, or at least a half day, where you can do what you want without interruption from anyone who makes your life difficult. If you need someone to baby-sit, find one and pay them well to show how much you appreciate that person.

I recently interviewed Mary Gordon at the Betty Ford Center. She heads up the family program and they have a good one. This is a week long program which covers the medical aspects of alcoholism, learning how to deal with the stress of living with an alcoholic, finding yourself in the chaos, learning to accept and let go by grieving your loss and moving on, and, creating a plan. Basically, the center covers just about everything I would want to know if I were a participant.

Someone once told me I was just as sick as Riley. This person didn't mean to be derogatory, but rather they wanted to point out that my mental and physical health had deteriorated since I began taking care of him. That person was right. Since I started this journey I have had or now have, a heart attack, stroke, flu (twice), salmonella (twice), insomnia, weight gain, diabetes, and general feelings of malaise. Yes, I agree, I am not as healthy as I wish I were.

I should have gone to a place like Betty Ford when I first decided to take him back in. But I didn't because I had been privileged enough to be a part of a military sponsored family program back in the 80's. It was intense and extremely educational. Fortunately, I had retained much of what I had previously learned. But, still it took me a while to get on even footing.

What has saved me from insanity is writing this blog. Writing has always been a passion that I've had since childhood. Writing this blog has re-kindled my need to write because I just can't NOT write. It is my passion. It has always been there, but work and the general business of living put in a box in my brain and ended up getting buried in the maze. Thanks to taking on this task with Riley, I've once again found the box and after opening it, the contents are flowing out like lava from a volcano.

Of course, it took me about a year to get to taking the cover off that box. If I had gone to the Betty Ford Center, maybe I would have opened the box long ago. I know that the health issues I have are easier to manage when I have an outlet for my frustration. There are things I can't "un-do" like the heart attack and stroke, but I now do more to prevent them from reoccurring. When I feel the stress from Riley's ridiculous-ness, I write it all down – I don't always publish it – but I get it out and find some perspective.

CHAPTER 12

DETACHMENT

The definition of the word "detachment" according to my big blue Webster's that resides on my shelf:

1. the action or process of detaching or separating; 2. aloofness or being unconcerned

There are others listed, but these are the ones that I feel are the most relevant to being involved with an alcoholic.

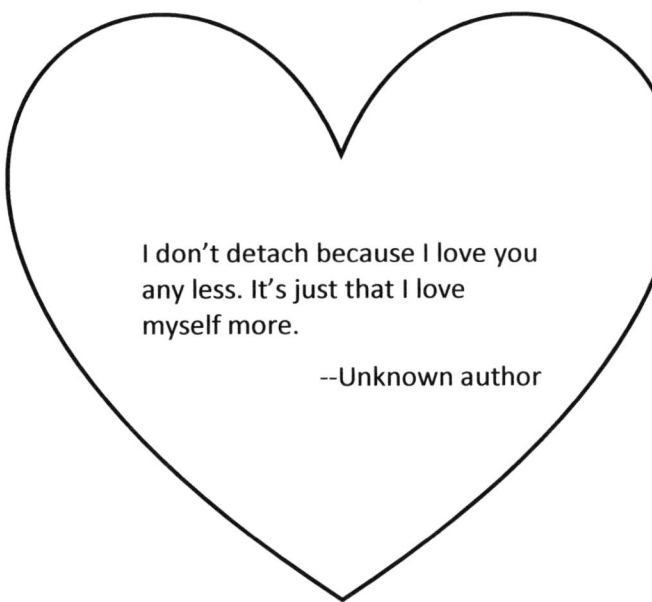

I don't detach because I love you any less. It's just that I love myself more.

--Unknown author

Although something that all caregivers must learn to do, it is the undoubtedly the most difficult and unnatural requirement. We are born into this world as an extension of other human beings. We interact and become part of all those around us. When we meet that "special" someone we vow to God in front of the world that as a couple we will become ONE and live the rest of our lives as a unit.

But then, alcohol comes along and inserts it's insidious self between the couple thereby separating the unit. While one party of the couple tries to maintain the "couple-ness" by remaining involved all every single segment of the alcoholic's world the other's mind is separated from the unit and only cares about their own tunnel vision focus.

In order to survive, the non-alcoholic person must compartmentalize the alcoholic life from the non-alcoholic life. The alcoholic thoughts, ideas, activities must be in their own compartment which will not interfere with the non-alcoholic's. While in the past the alcoholic was once the most important person in the non-alcoholic's life, the priority has shifted and the non-alcoholic must replace the alcoholic in order of importance.

The alcoholism belongs to the alcoholic. It is not yours to resolve, manage or cure. It is not in your compartment so let it go. Become aloof to what the alcoholic needs, wants or believes.

Let me make this clear. You may be the caregiver and if your alcoholic is at a point where he can no-longer take care of him/herself, then you may have decided to take care of his basic needs for him. You must decide how much you will do and how you will handle the tasks. Will you hire someone to come in or will you do it yourself? If you have the financial means, hire someone. If you decide to do it yourself, don't get caught up in making it the only thing you have to do. Be like a janitor – do what needs to be done and punch the time clock as "out". Do not get caught up in long conversations or taking orders. Don't muddle your compartment with smudges of the alcoholic.

Taking care of the alcoholic doesn't mean you can't have your own life. If you detach, or become aloof / mentally separate from the alcoholic, you can have a life of your own. If you don't know what you would do with this new found life, go back to Chapter 9 Discover Yourself and refresh your memory about who you are and what things you enjoy doing.

You can survive your role as caregiver. You can be happy and have a wonderful life. But you must master the art of detachment in order to be happy and successful.

Dead? Alive?
From Immortal Alcoholic blog post dated February 17, 2013

This was written by an OARS member who is the daughter of an alcoholic. She has chosen to take a step back from her father as he walks down his alcoholic path. The invisible umbilical cord binding child to parent still remains as she tries to minimize her involvement in his insane behavior. In my opinion, she has mastered the art of detaching with love.

Ms Forland writes:

I don't go to my alcoholic father's house as much as I used to… but do pass it on the way to work. I phone him often to "check in" but when I don't get an answer a knot forms in my stomach and won't go away until I hear from or see him. This week it was about two or three days and since he had received his check for his pension recently, I figured he was on a bender.

Dead or Alive? Dead or Alive? Those thoughts keep going through my head as I drove to his house a few days ago.

I shoveled his driveway and steps and was comforted to see footprints in the snow leading to his door. I could not bring myself to actually go into the house. I figured he was plastered or dead, or in bed asleep since he sleeps all day and drinks all night.

The next day, I couldn't handle the stomach pains from the anxiety of not knowing if he was dead or alive, so I went to his house again. As I walked up to the door, I threw salt on the steps and waited to see if the front door would open on its own. It did not.

I walked in, paused and listened for sounds of life. Both the TVs were on full blast. Dead or Alive? I slowly walked through the kitchen. The counters and table were cluttered with empty bottles of rum and vodka among the food and dirty dishes. Dead or Alive? I entered the living room, some papers were scattered everywhere along with plates of food on the floor. There was no sign of him on the main floor. No blood or vomit. Good sign, right?

Dead or Alive? Dead or Alive?

Upstairs, I pause and listen. Quiet. Dead or Alive? I took a deep breath and slowly walked to his bedroom. Dead or Alive? I turn the corner and can see into his room. TADA! There he is. I see his body move slightly and I know he is still alive. I sneak backwards out of the room, turn and go down the stairs and, quietly but quickly, out the door.

As I drove home, I could feel my stomach knots unravel and relax. I'm good. That is until the next time.

Detaching is one of the hardest things ever needed when someone we love is addicted to alcohol or drugs. The problem seems to be more complicated when detachment is needed between children and parents or vice versa. I always have the option of leaving and forgetting about my husband, but it never feels like an option for a parent to leave a child or a child to leave a parent. Those ties cannot be cut by a bunch of legal words on a court-recorded document. The ties are binding for life.

I admire Ms Forland for finding a way to satisfy her need to protect him and, at the same time, protect herself. I know that what she wanted to do was wake him up and shake some sense into him. I know I would have had a hard time resisting that urge. I admire her for not cleaning up his house, stocking his refrigerator with healthy food and thereby letting him believe she will take care of his messes. She was able to recognize HER need to know if he was still alive and once that need was met she did nothing more. Nothing more would have done anyone any good or made her feel any better.

If the person had been her child, I think it would have been even harder for her to walk out the door. It's so extremely hard to keep those maternal protection instincts from kicking in and trying to save the child from imminent danger. Sometimes trying to save the child in that moment only teaches them they can depend on the parent to always come to their rescue. That in turn prevents them from actually taking responsibility for themselves and saving their own lives.

I think it's normal for each of us to think we would know what we would do if we were placed into a certain situation. The fact is that we never really know how we will react or what we would do. There are so many scenarios to life, it's impossible to imagine every which way we would turn in the real event. Sometimes we just react instinctively and other times we think things through to a rational end. The main thing to remember is that no matter what we do, we will always do what we feel is the right thing in whatever the circumstance and in that instant. It may not seem right to others, or in my own hindsight, but there is no need to feel guilty or accept others criticism. Pushing down those feelings of guilt are sometimes harder than doing what you felt was right at the time.

As for me, I fight the "guilt-monster" every single day. But, I am confident I've always done what I felt was the best thing to do at any given time and in any given circumstance based on the information at hand and from my previous experiences. To do any less would be like trying to revive the Pansies I planted last spring.

CHAPTER 13

CO-DEPENDENCE

This will be the chapter that I hate writing. I dislike the word "co-dependent". I dislike being described as co-dependent. While it may not have intended to be, I always feel that I'm being a bit disrespected when someone says I'm co-dependent. I feel belittled because the term indicates that I am not a person unto myself. That I'm only a part of someone else and without that person I do not exist.

In fact, I AM co-dependent on my alcoholic but for that not to leave a bad taste in my mouth I must break down the term "co-dependent".

In my opinion, all married / partnered couples are dependent on each other making them co-dependent. Anytime anyone works hand in hand with another person or persons, they are co-dependent. Being co-dependent is not always a bad situation. I'd rather call it team-work than co-dependence.

> Don't change who you are in order to be what someone else needs.
> --Author Unknown

My relationship with Riley has always been one of "co-dependence". We started as a team and ended up as co-dependents.

I am dependent on him to provide me with fodder for my blog and books. I depend on him to provide me with inspiration to do research and investigation into anything concerning alcoholism. Our finances are joined, so I'm dependent on him financially. However, I am only co-dependent in as much as I need to be in order to have a path to my survival. My co-dependence of him has led to me becoming, in a sense, independent. If Riley ceased to exist, I would still be doing exactly what I'm doing now.

Unfortunately, most times when the co-dependent title is used, it means that for some reason one person is dependent on another to continue an undesirable behavior because it gives the caregiver a purpose, happiness, and/or security. For some reason, the caregiver needs the alcoholic to continue being drunk or create problems that the caregiver can resolve.

I never needed Riley to be drunk in order to maintain my happiness. In fact, I didn't need Riley at all in order to be happy. If I was in need of being reminded that there was happiness anywhere, I didn't have to look any further than my own family. My kids, parents, siblings and friends was all in need to find purpose and love. Riley was supposed to be the cherry on top of my happiness sundae. But cherries roll off and I don't really miss it at all. I keep my sundaes simple – toasted pound cake, vanilla ice cream, hot fudge sauce and whipped cream – no cherry.

When someone describes you as being co-dependent, don't take it to heart. Don't think that person is being disrespectful. Just remember that you don't really need a cherry on top of your sundae. And your only response should be "OK", or anything else that would acknowledge what they said without really agreeing with the comment.

Co-Dependent – A dirty word?
From Immortal Alcoholic blog dated October 24, 2015

In my opinion, marriage is a co-dependent relationship. That's the way it should be. The couple depends on each other as a unit in order for tasks to be completed or simply to make life easier for each other. Co-dependency works for marriages. Co-dependency is not a dirty word.

I read somewhere (I can't remember where) that anyone who is involved with an alcoholic is most likely co-dependent. Well, that's kinda like saying most skinny people do not like chocolate. I know lots of skinny people who absolutely adore chocolate just like I know spouses, parents, siblings, and friends of alcoholics who are not dependent on keeping the alcoholic drunk.

The word co-dependent seems to have been tossed around so much that we could just do away with "wife", "brother", "father" and any other relationship status titles. Kleenex is a tissue, but instead of saying "we need a box of tissue," we often say "we need a box of Kleenex." The name Kleenex has become the household word for tissue. The title co-dependent has become the household word for anyone related to an alcoholic.

What does it mean to be co-dependent anyway? Wikipedia defines co-dependent relationships as a "type of dysfunctional helping relationship where one person supports or enables another person's addiction."

OK. I agree with the definition. I agree that there are people who depend on the drunkenness of their mate in order to get what they need. It may be that the way to get grocery money is to wait for the alcoholic to pass out and they take the alcoholic's wallet. It may be that the alcoholic is more agreeable to suggestions of the spouse if he/she is snockered. It could even be that the only way the spouse feels like a part of a couple is for the alcoholic to NEED him or her – to drive them home or clean up their messes – which makes them a team and it could be the only way for one of the team to feel needed. I agree this is not healthy, but it could that to survive one must make the other believe they are truly needed.

I don't agree that the title of co-dependent should be a blanket description for all people involved with an alcoholic. I believe there are far more people who trying to survive the outfall of the alcoholic behavior by any means possible. Most people do not depend on the lack of sobriety of their spouse, but they do have to find ways to work around it.

Personally the word "co-dependent" feels like an accusation. It is as though I have poured the bottle down Riley's throat in order to keep him drunk. It feels that I am somehow to blame for his demise. I can tell you that alcoholics do not need help getting drunk, they can manage that all on their own. So let's stop blaming the people around the alcoholic and place it back on the shoulders of the person who is really to blame for their situation – the alcoholic.

It also occurs to me that the ones calling the sober partners "co-dependent" are often the alcoholics whether they are in recovery or not. It's a scapegoat for them. "I can't recover because my wife is co-dependent and wants me to keep drinking." Hogwash.

I have never heard from any of my readers that they have a need for the alcoholic to continue drinking. It has always been the opposite. My readers want the alcoholic in their life to stop drinking and return to a healthy lifestyle. No one is ever happy about someone they love vomiting all over the sofa, or, smelling like a garbage can. No one ever tells themselves in the morning that "It's going to be a wonderful day because my wife will probably put dish soap on the pancakes."

Everything changes when the alcoholic reaches end-stage. Rules and blanket descriptions just do not fit. By this time, it's simply a matter of keeping your head above water in whatever manner necessary. It doesn't matter what labels or titles other people may assign to you. I'm sure they mean well, but it doesn't mean they are right. You are the only one who has to live with yourself when this phase finally reaches its end. If you need help, seek advice from someone who has walked in your footprints. If you have not lived life with an end-stage alcoholic, you have no idea what you're talking about.

Let me perfectly clearn – I absolutely do believe that co-dependency in alcoholic relationships actual does exist. I do not believe every relationship with an alcoholic is co-dependent. I believe it's not the place of one person to label another.

CHAPTER 14

SUPPORT GROUPS

Never underestimate the value of support groups. Talking with others who share your situation can help determine your next move; provide consolation; and develop relationships with understanding individuals. Remember the old saying, "There's strength in numbers."? It may be an old saying, but there is truth in those words. Increasing your circle of friends will provide you with encouragement as well as giving you a person to do things with – like going to a movie or going for a walk. You may already have a large circle of friends and that's OK. But these new friends are important because they give you a different perspective to your situation. Treasure your current friends and create new ones who will eventually will be golden.

> **Two heads are better than one.**
> *--Proverb*

My primary issue with support groups, and most recovery center family programs, is that they have a tendency help the family learn how to help the alcoholic. The alcoholic must own his/her disease, situation, and/or problems. It's not the family's responsibility to help the alcoholic. It IS the family's responsibility to find recovery for themselves as individuals. Here's the accidental benefit to not focusing on the alcoholic – the alcoholic starts to focus on the alcoholic because the attention from the family is no longer there. If they can't get what they need from a non-alcoholic, they must provide for it themselves.

I imagine that the first thing that sprang to your mind when you read "support groups" was Al-Anon. While I am not always in agreement with the tenets of Al-Anon, I think there is a lot to be gained from attending a meeting when you feel in need of others involved with alcoholism. You can always "take what you like/need and leave the rest". The great thing about Al-Anon is that you may meet someone with whom you can relate. You might hear something you needed to hear. My advice is to try going to a meeting here and there in different locations. You may find something that fits for you. Then again you may not. Don't force it upon yourself. If you're not comfortable, move Al-Anon to your resource bag and move on.

Smart Recovery doesn't have physical meetings everywhere, but they do have on-line meetings. Check their website http://www.smartrecovery.org/ for more information. This is actually support for alcoholics and addicts, however, they welcome family and friends as well.

OARS Group (Our Alcoholism Resource and Support) is for family and friends of end-stage alcoholics. The end-stage part is not a requirement; any stage of alcoholism is accepted even if the alcoholic is no longer among the living.

There is a FaceBook "Secret" page where the conversation is lively and people connect easily. This group is "secret" to allow the members to speak freely and not be judged by others may not have any experience with alcoholism. If you're an avid FaceBook person, this may be the group for you.

There is an OARS website at www.OARSFamilySupport.weebly.com which was set up to accommodate everyone including those who do not use FaceBook. There is a place on this site that allows for Live Chat. This site holds a lot of information and is good even if you don't use it to reach out to others. Just reading what others have written will provide some support. This site is still in the early stages. As the number of members grow, the activity will increase allowing for more conversations and more subjects.

For FaceBook, you must e-mail me your e-mail address and I'll send you an invitation to join. For the OARSFamilySupport, you must subscribe to the site. There is a $5 monthly fee but the first month is free. This is similar to passing the hat at any AlAnon meeting.

Another avenue to consider is one-on-one counseling. Google the name of a therapist you would like to use and see what pops up. You are looking for a person who has extensive experience in alcohol and substance abuse. If you have no insurance, try your local health department. Often they have resources to help get counseling either through them or outside sources.

The key to this type of counseling is to be as open and honest as you can possibly be. Nothing will shock a good therapist and they can't help if they don't truly understand your situation.

If you can afford it or find it, call the local rehab centers and ask about their family programs. Ask if you may attend even though your alcoholic is not a patient. Sometimes centers will allow people to go to their program solo. Your insurance probably will not cover it, but it is worth a try to call the insurance company and ask if it would be covered. After all, counseling is usually covered and this would just be a more intensive type of therapy.

They are very difficult to find, but recovery coaches are popping up everywhere now a days. Most are for the addicted person, but keep searching until you find one that works for you. I offer one-on-one coaching for family and friends only. You can book a session with me by e-mailing me and setting up a convenient time for a telephone conversation.

CHAPTER 15

RESOURCES

www.OARSFamilySupport.weebly.com (There is a $5 monthly subscription fee to this forum.) In this forum setting you will find non-judgmental support, useful information and answers to your questions.

FaceBook OARS F&F Group (This is a "secret" group. You must send an e-mail to ImmortalAlcoholic@gmail.com and request an invitation to the group.

Al-Anon and www.AlAnon.org; Adult Children of Alcoholics – There is an extensive on-line support network. Simply Google AlAnon.

http://www.smartrecovery.org/resources/family.htm

www.about.alcoholism.com

www.recoverymonth.gov

www.soberrecovery.com

Learn to Cope, an extensive peer support network offering support to family members of alcoholics. They are based in Massachusetts but have an on-line support program.

PAL Group (Parents of Addicted Loved Ones) which was originally based in Arizona, it has spread to several other states and has an on-line network.

There are numerous blogs that focus on the family side of alcoholism:

Immortal Alcoholic by Linda Doyne

Quiet Raging Waters by Wren Waters

Alcoholic Daze – by Addy

For general and medical information about alcoholism, visit the below sites:

http://alcoholism.about.com/lr/health_effects_of_alcohol

www.wikipedia.org/wiki

www.niaaa.nih.gov

Recovery For All
From Immortal Alcoholic blog dated September 15, 2011

September is **National Recovery Month**. When I hear about recovery, my mind is always drawn to the alcoholic or addict that has entered a rehab center. It is a step in the direction of sanity and the most difficult for them to take. But, recovery isn't just for the one imbibing on substance or alcohol abuse. The entire family needs recovery as well.

Many end-stage caregivers get here by accident. We don't get married and say... "I'm so happy eventually I'll be able clean up the vomit and poop left by my alcoholic soul mate." No new mother says... "Oh my baby is beautiful! And someday his skin will be florescent yellow and you won't be able to see the whites of his eyes! What a joy that will be!" Or what about the child who writes a school essay with a title of "When I Grew Up I Want to be a Drunk Like My Mom!"

Most of us don't even know that alcoholism will be a part of our lives at all. Many of us deny it's a factor even when it begins to show its face. We go along living our happy lives. We make detours along the way — we revise, reinvent, regroup, redirect and then it hits us that our direction is leading to a place we did not intend to go. It all happens so slowly that we don't see it until it may be too late.

OK. The question isn't HOW we got here but rather what we do now. This thing called addiction is a tough thing to understand and many people spend years in institutions of higher learning to get a grasp on understanding. We family members don't have time for that. We must use other resources. Fortunately, those OTHER resources do exist.

If your alcoholic goes into rehab, ask the center about their family program. If they have one, take advantage of it. Attend with an open mind. Take in every bit of knowledge they offer. Most family programs are simply an extension of Al-Anon and that is unfortunate because there is so much more the family needs to know. But, whatever is offered should not be refused. It is a starting place and just that — a place to start adding to your knowledge database. **Education and knowledge is the key to surviving alcoholic insanity**. Let it begin here.

If you alcoholic **isn't** going into rehab, do some research by calling around to different rehab centers. Ask if they offer a family program if the alcoholic is **not** a patient at their center. Many centers offer these programs and are usually covered under most insurance plans. Ask what is covered in their program. Do they include medical facts, how the disease progresses, or details of the family dynamics? They should always include an introduction to the Al-Anon experience. Find the center that offers the most information.

Now that you've got the basics out of the way start going to Al-Anon. The Al-Anon doctrine doesn't always fit for the caregivers of end-stage alcoholics, but it provides an excellent platform for anyone dealing with alcoholism on any level. You will find within those meetings other people who may have similar difficulties and others who have yet to face what you've encountered. There is a support system in those meetings that you won't find anywhere else. They all know the depth of your despair. They all keep the same secrets as you. There is strength in numbers and this is where family members can begin building their support systems. Families of alcoholics cannot depend solely on each other for support because other family members are subjective in their points of view. The objectivity of outsiders can often bring things into focus and provide alternatives to seemingly hopeless situations. If you can't get to a real live meeting, there are meetings on-line.

This is the information age and we are fortunate enough to have computers. Research every aspect of alcoholism. Learn every thing you can about what alcohol does to the body, how it progresses and how it affects every member of the family. Google the names of diseases and complications such as cirrhosis and hepatic encephalopathy. Become your own walking reference section. The more you know, the less shocked you will be by the changes in the active alcoholic's mind and body. **Knowledge is the key to survival.**

Below are just a few of the excellent sources of factual medical information:

http://alcoholism.about.com/lr/health_effects_of_alcohol

www.wikipedia.org/wiki

www.niaaa.nih.gov

There are lots of resources out there. Search by the bodily organ or name of the complication. If you simply enter "end-stage alcoholism" you will not end up with very many relevant leads. If you just search "alcoholism" you will be overwhelmed with an endless possibility of websites.

Connect with others. This blog offers support and information to end-stage caregivers, but there are other blogs. I use my personal experiences to show others that they are not alone in this insanity. Different blogs offer different points of view and different means of getting their point across. Visit them often and discover your favorites. Add yourself to the list of "Followers" to show your support for the efforts of the blog author. My favorites are listed on the left side of my blog page, but I do read others that are not listed here.

I have a FACEBOOK page where there is often a lively running **"conversation"** *on a variety of subjects. This is where you can develop relationships with other readers who may be walking in your shoes. Ask questions and everyone will give you their own opinion and suggestion. It's an open discussion on any topic.*

Interaction can also be found on other sites such as www.about.alcoholism.com, www.recoverymonth.gov, and/or www.soberrecovery.com. These sites offer forums that allow readers to connect and offer various points of view.

*Twitter also offers support. This service allows you to follow others who may share your difficulties. I have a Twitter account (which is FREE) and have found it be a helpful resource. There are many rehab centers, counselors, groups, etc. that connect using this site. For anyone interested I am **ImrtlAlkysWife** on Twitter.*

My point here is simple. *No one is an island. No one is immune. Anyone involved with an alcoholic on any level is subject to distorted thinking, unrealistic expectations and a whole host of difficult situations which can even lead to our own physical ailments. We need to become sane again. We need help to get back on the path to a healthy lifestyle.* **We need recovery** *just as much – or maybe even more – than the alcoholic no matter what the stage.*

CHAPTER 16

WHEN THE FAT LADY SINGS

It ain't over 'til the fat lady sings!

During this journey through the alcoholic chaos, there will be times when you will say "Oh God, just let him go. Take him and give me some peace." But he/she may appear to immortal because they keep recovering and starting the process over and over again. It seem there will never be an end to all the chaos.

Eventually there will come a time when the alcoholic will pass on to the great liquor bar in heaven. It's probably in some tropical setting with everyone sitting around in lounge chairs being served by beautiful/handsome attendants. Oh…. Back to the subject.

When the alcoholic does pass there may be some confusion as to what to say, how to feel, what to do, etc. There are no simple answers. If you emotionally separated yourself from the alcoholic before his demise, then you're one step up. If you are still emotionally attached, things will be more complicated. It's OK. You're going to get through it.

There are other people who will mourn the death and will not be as objective as you. The best thing you can say is almost nothing. Nod your head and smile or give a little frown. Tell people that you already are missing him/her. (The fact is you started missing the person the alcoholic was for quite some time already.) Say something nice – there must have been something nice about the person or you would never have become attached.

If there are children, you must remember that no matter what, he was their Dad or she was their Mother. You don't have to tell children all the bad things about their parents. They probably know a lot more than you think they know. So upon the death, focus on the positive things the parent did with the children. They will come to form their own opinions as they get older, but let them be kids for just a little while longer.

On the practical side there are some things you should know. First, there is an organization called "MedCure". They will take the remains and thoroughly examine it. After the extensive autopsy, they will cremate the body and return it to you. There is no cost to the family for this. If you are having difficulty paying for the services, this can be an alternative.

If the alcoholic was a veteran, check with the Veterans Administration to find out what they offer to help with the final arrangements. They will do a honor guard if requested. Don't expect much, if any monetary assistance. But, for example, Riley's ashes will be taken aboard a submarine and he will be buried at sea.

Social Security will not be sending you a windfall either. I believe the death benefit is about $250 and hasn't increased in years.

Memorial services can be held anywhere, in a park, church reception hall, at a home or anywhere that you feel comfortable. If money is an issue – and really, isn't it always – have a potluck dinner or dessert tasting. Keep it simple.

Don't be surprised when you find yourself grieving for the alcoholic. It is not the person he became that you are longing for. It is the person without the alcohol infused brain that has created a void. You knew he was gone long ago, but now it's real. It's final. There are no possibilities of recovery or chances to make things right. Let yourself go through all the phases. There's nothing wrong with you except that you are normal.

Til death do us part
From Immortal Alcoholic blog dated November 23, 2016

I hate it when I get e-mails from people who have lost a loved one to alcoholism. My heart breaks for them and all I want is to hold them like a baby to ease the pain. I remember the unbearable stabbing in my heart when Captain Morgan stole my son from me.

I slugged my way through the memorial service with fake smiles and nods as loving friends and family took my hand and told me how sorry they were. My mind raced with sarcastic comments – they weren't as sorry as I was and NO, I didn't believe he was better off now. Instead I simply nodded and said "Thank you for coming."

My older brother died of leukemia. I had the same feeling when he died that I did when my son died. Leukemia stole my brother and I didn't think he was now in a much better place. His place was with me and my other brothers. His place was on one of his barges or wheeling and dealing some buy-sell transaction. He was not supposed to be in a pretty box in the ground.

I suppose I feel the same way when anyone I love passes. The initial grief of losing a loved one is overwhelming. It takes me a while to calm down and accept what the truth.

What the other mourners are saying is that they feel my loss as well. Sometimes it doesn't They aren't being disrespectful. They are showing their love in whatever way they can.

I am grateful for all those who expressed their condolences. It was comforting to be able to see how many people loved my son and my brother. The fact that they simply attended and told him goodbye meant a lot to me. I looked around the room and knew he would be missed.

There were rumblings and discussions of Captain Morgan and what a shame it was that my son's life was wasted. Those discussions were not directed at me very often. If they had been I would have responded with, WASTED? My son's life was not wasted. It was cut short but not wasted. I would remind them that he had done a lot of good things, interesting things, productive things during the short time he was on the earth.

Just because someone is addicted to something doesn't mean that person doesn't have value. What about all the years when they weren't an alcoholic? And sometimes they continue to be a productive member of society while also getting into the deeper throes of the bottle.

Alcoholics are a person first and not just an alcoholic. There are people who love this alcoholic person. They are someone's spouse, parent, sibling, friend even if they may have become estranged as the disease progressed. The memories remain from days before.

The next time you have the misfortune to attend a memorial service, celebration of life, homegoing, funeral… whatever term you use… Instead of saying the deceased is no longer in pain try instead saying something positive about the person. "Your son (mother, father, sister, brother) was a loving person and I'll miss his beautiful smile." OR "Your father could be quite a rascal. I'll miss his mischievousness." You can even say "Your brother lived on the edge. He had an interesting life."

I know that alcoholics create havoc, can be mean and not loving at all. Their value system fails and it seems that no one will miss them when they are gone. The fact is no one will miss the alcohol part of the person, but someone will miss the PERSON he was without the alcohol.

Once a person is gone it's time to take alcohol inspired memories, put them in a box and hide the box away. Someday when the pain subsides, take them out and you can either laugh or cry. Then put them back in the box and burn it. It's over. It's done.

CHAPTER 17

MY FAVORITE BLOG POSTS

Most of these blog posts are from the Immortal Alcoholic blog. There are a couple of other blogs and I've identified them for you. I hope you enjoy these postings.

Jury Duty
From Immortal Alcoholic blog dated January 20, 2014

Jury Duty is one of the responsibilities of being a member of our society. It may be inconvenient and feel like an intrusion on our life, but it is necessary. Anyone chosen for the jury duty process of selection should take the event seriously. The following was overheard as I waited for to be granted entrance into the courtroom. People were being screened through the metal detector. There were two bailiffs involved in the procedure.

First Bailiff: "Are you drunk?"

Potential Juror: "No. I'm Ashley." She held out a very shaky hand to the Bailiff, but he rebuffed the salutation. Ms Ashley's mother stood next to her with a support hand at the back center of her daughter's waist. She would have been voted as the best dressed juror in comparison to the other candidates. She wore a beautiful blue knit dress with a leather belt in the same color blue. Her hair looked as though she had just come from the beauty salon. Her makeup was flawlessly applied yet subtle. She could have been a politician's wife on the campaign trail. But the swaying and shaking of her body told a tell that the togetherness of her exterior did not match her interior.

Second Bailiff: "What's in your drinking glass, Ms. Ashley?"

Ms Ashley: "It's OK. It's just water."

Second Bailiff: "You won't be able to take that glass into the courtroom."

Ms Ashley: "It's OK. It's just water."

Ms Ashley walked away (with the aide of her mother) tottering on her high heels.

First Bailiff to Second Bailiff: "We'll have to do a breathalyzer on her. She's smelly of the stuff."

Second Bailiff to First Bailiff: "I agree. Let's get a female officer down here."

About ten minutes later, a female officer arrived and there was a conversation about what would happen if the results were over the legal limit. She would be arrested. They spoke quietly, but the small lobby made it impossible to carry on a private conversation.

Riley looked up at me and said, "So what if she's been drinking. It doesn't mean she wouldn't be a good juror." I proceeded to explain to him that jurors in to be in a clear state of mind so that they would understand the facts of the case presented. "It's not illegal to drink," he said. "So she's had a few. It's OK." I didn't respond.

Now that the posse had been assembled and measures / counter-measures were in place, the First Bailiff went outside to find Ms Ashley. She was not there, but her mother was. Her mother explained that she only had that odor because she had been drinking constantly over the past three weeks. But, she had not been drinking that morning and therefore she was not drunk. The First Bailiff explained that she could not be allowed into the courtroom if she was above the legal limit on the test.

Ms Ashley appeared from the ladies room and said she had no idea why they would want to do a breathalyzer on her. Her comment was directed to an innocent, handsome, male by-stander. "Are you kidding me??? You reek of a distillery!" He exclaimed and then walked away from her. She muttered "Asshole" under her breath, but everyone in the lobby could still hear her.

The posse came over to her and said they needed to take the test. Ms Ashley informed them that she did not want to take the test, but would speak to her attorney who just happened to be in court that day. The lawyer came from around the corner where Ms Ashley stopped him and told him she did not want to take the test. The lawyer shared a few words with the bailiffs. It took less than five minutes for the lawyer to turn right back around and tell Ms Ashley to wait an hour or so and then take the test. She left to go outside to have a cigarette.

It was about 30 minutes later when the lawyer came up to the bailiffs and asked if they had gone ahead and taken her into custody. They told him no. He said he could not find Ms Ashley or her mother anywhere on the grounds. Someone in the background said – "She said she was leaving. She said she wasn't going to stick around for this bull shit, got in her car and drove off. She wouldn't let her mother drive. They were arguing." The bailiff's thakedn the informant and then notified the police of a potential drunk driver by the name of Ashley etc., etc.

I don't know what happened to the woman and her mother. Shortly after all the drama, we were informed that we could all go home. Well, it was an entertaining morning anyway.

I wonder how many people show up for court appearances while they are still in the midst of foggy-mindedness. I bet it is more than I had ever anticipated. The thought of being a defendant with the question of my freedom on the line – and having my fate determined by someone who obviously is not of sound mind – is more than irritating, it's downright frightful.

Should all jurors be given a breathalyzer before entering the courtroom? It seems logical to me. On the other hand, it could be construed as a violation of a person's civil rights. After all, an occasional drink in the morning doesn't make you an alcoholic. Or does it?

For me, it's not so much about determining if a person is an alcoholic. It's more about having the good sense NOT to drink when you know you will be in a situation of having power over another person's life. If I were on trial, I would prefer all my jurors be blessed with sound judgment and sober minds.

How happiness feels
From the Immortal Alcoholic blog dated May 14, 2014

I woke up feeling especially grateful this morning. I'm up before the sunrise on a normal day, but today I was up and ready to go do whatever was on my list for today. AND there are lots of items on my list!

Yesterday Riley had an appointment at the medical doctors and he has ordered a neurological exam as well as a complete heart workup. This may lead to getting some help in the way of a home health aide or, maybe even, a placement in a facility. The appointment was more than an hour long and by the time it was over, the doctor was just as confused as I usually am. It was a good way to spend that hour.

I felt relieved that Carrot has made such an amazing turn for the better. Her surgery and my not being able to be there put a giant dark cloud over my head. I have talked to her and others have gone to see her and now she may be kicking around this world even longer than her kids!

Carrot's daughter is her caregiver and is dealing with her own crisis involving her husband's health. But, a couple of people have stepped up and made an effort to provide some assistance. I am especially grateful for their support. I wish more family members would take the initiative to drop off a casserole or pick up a prescription or do a bit of grocery shopping.

But, that's another story for another time.

I am grateful for having a new mentor in my life that is encouraging and supporting me to go forward with projects that I had simply pushed off into the far reaches of my brain. Her experience is beyond reproach and her faith in me is almost scary. When asked to help produce the documentary on alcoholism, I knew Riley's story would not fit the criteria, but thought this to be such a beneficial project, I was determined to participate. I didn't know the reward would come to me in the form of renewed self-confidence and determination within my own being.

Another recent surprise is how much my health has improved in just a month. I find myself waking up in the morning with a clear brain and focus. I no longer feel rushed to get every chore done by noon because I burn out by the time the noon whistle blows. I'm able to go outside and work in the flower beds or herb garden. My diabetes is completely under control. I no longer allow myself to be pressured to fix a 4-course dinner for Riley every evening. Several times during the week he simply gets a sandwich or TV dinner. If I feel that I am in pain or tired, I have no remorse in taking a nap or resting. I've lost a little weight, my blood pressure is not in the danger levels and I have a sense of regaining my health.

When my eyes opened this morning I felt so thankful for having the "besties" in my life that I have. There are three women in my life who know about the skeletons in my closet and they purposely have lost the key. Even when having "issues" we are still best friends. How could I NOT be thankful for that?

I got up, poured a cup of coffee, unloaded the dishwasher, made a meat loaf for dinner, and racked my brain for a name for the one-on-one coaching sessions that I hope will start as early as next week. I let the dog out and the cat in. I tried to have a conversation with Riley. I then locked myself in my office and started writing this post.

Of course, my life is still very difficult but for the first time in a very long time, I don't feel as though I'm just surviving each day. For the first morning in many mornings, I woke up feeling useful. I have people to help and public speaking events to plan as well as getting my book into paperback medium. I have potential documentary stories to review and evaluate.

I wish I could reach out to each of you and give you a bit of the goodness I'm feeling today. I wish I had the power to touch you on the shoulder and transfer a bit of light into your world. I don't know for how long I will have the feeling of comfort, maybe for a day or maybe just a few hours, but however long it lasts I want to make the most of it.

I am a lucky girl because for today, right this minute, I remember how happiness feels. Today I am happy.

Bootstraps
From Immortal Alcoholic blog dated February 21, 2015

Lately, I seem to be dealing with a lot of people who have gone through some really – I mean REALLY – tough times. Every idea, thought, dream, confidence is being tested and the result is that they are having difficulty trusting in their own abilities. They have lost a sense of

self which has created low self-esteem. Each and every one of these people who have always been self-confident, problem-solvers, often gave advice to others on how to improve the other person's life. The spark seems to be out of feeding flint. There's no little bundle of fuzz to help catch the spark into a blaze. Something is wrong.

Many times over the years, I could relate to the above paragraph. Many times I have said I was just going to walk away from everything that appeared to be creating a problem including the blog, the support groups, my husband, the house, and even, my dog and cat. I know. I know. Running away is never the answer. But, when things seem to "not be fixable" and I can't figure out what to do, I doubt my abilities to finish or DO whatever needs to be done. My self-confidence is trampled upon until it's just as flat as a critter run over by an 18-wheeler.

I can hear my mother telling me to "get over it" and to "pick yourself up by the bootstraps and get on with it", and (my personal favorite) "if you aren't solving the problem then you ARE the problem." Phew!! My mother was a great believer in using a work-around system to try and try again. If one thing didn't work, try a different approach, make a new plan, but don't ever quit.

Although a bit drill-sargent-y-ish, I think my mother was right. Mother's always seem more right as we get on in years. Wish I had listened to her more when I was in my 30s rather than waiting til my 60s.

Anyway, I believe there are ways to build our self-esteem after a devastating disaster in our lives. One of the most common is to seek professional help. A good therapist can go a long way to making us understand that not every loss or fail is a sign that we are not competent.

I have some simpler things that I often do when I start to feel defeated. I go to the salon and get pampered a bit. Invite a friend and after the makeover go for coffee, dinner, or anything that is out of the ordinary. A physical change can sometimes led to a mental change.

Do something physical. Go for a walk, swim, or to the gym for a nice sweaty workout. While improving your health you can improve your state-of-mind. I find that when I'm walking I often let my mind wander and sometimes it strikes upon a solution to my *current issue. I don't consciously seek the answer, I just let my mind go and do its own thing.*

For a financial issue, I get advice from my banker or anyone who knows and understands accounting, budgets, etc. Maybe someone can help set up a budget or review the situation. When I'm totally stressed over not having enough money, I take a look at my own budget and see where I can cut expenses or how I can best pay the bills around my paydays. Sometimes I call the creditor and ask if some kind of arrangement can be made to help the situation.

Don't forget about the BIG bills. I constantly worried about the IRS until I called them and worked out a plan to get caught up on my back taxes. It was easier than I thought it would be and now I'm not thinking I'm a low life because I owe money to the government.

A friend of mine was fired from her job after 17 years of very loyal service. The firing had nothing to do with her job performance or ability. But, after being denied for unemployment and applying for jobs all over the state, she feels "unemployable" and "incompetent." She fears she will never work again in a field in which she has always excelled. I suggested that she go to a temp agency and take on simple assignments. That way her self-confidence might come back up to par. Maybe she could go back to school and take a few classes that would show her that she's capable of learning something new.

If you doubt your ability as a parent, re-evaluate your how you have handled parental crises in the past. Take a long hard look at your children and ask yourself: Are they healthy? Are they clean? Are they well-fed? Are they happy? Is there anything you would not do to keep them safe? If you feel you are doing the best you can, then that's all you can do. Don't ask anyone if you are a good parent. People have a tendency to tell you what they think you want to hear. This would be a great topic for that professional counselor that I was talking about earlier.

The most important thing about getting your mo-jo back is -- don't stop. Don't give up and let someone else's ideas run your life. Whatever it is that is making you feel inadequate is the thing you need to do more of. You might not succeed on the first couple of tries. But if you quit you will always feel as though you CAN'T do whatever the thing is. Instead just keep trying and telling yourself that you CAN. Tell yourself that often and soon you will believe it. Once you believe it, then you will DO what needs to be done. Think outside the box, get a new plan, and look at your options.

It isn't that you're not good enough or just can't, it's that just haven't found the key to your dilemma. Patiently try every key on the ring and eventually one will open the door.

Tuesday's Towel
From Immortal Alcoholic blog dated April 17, 2011

One of my very first needlecraft projects was to embroider a set of kitchen towels. My mother bought seven blank "flour sack" towels and ironed a transfer onto each one (do they even make those anymore?). The lines were to be stitched using bright colored embroidery thread in several different stitch styles. There were seven towels – one for each day of the week and each day had a specific task: Monday-Sweep; Tuesday-Dust; Wednesday-Laundry; Thursday-Ironing; Friday-Mend; Saturday-Shop; Sunday-Rest. It took me a while to get them completed, but I was sooooooo proud of them when they were all done and neatly hung on the handle of the oven. For months I changed them daily so they matched the appropriate day of the week.

My little girl mind would often drift into believing that maybe this is how life was supposed to be lived. Was there a day for each chore and was it always to be done consistently each and every week? I wondered if this was the way life was suppose to be lived and the fact that my family didn't operate in that manner meant that we were somehow not living the "right" way.

After a few months, I forgot about putting the right towel out for the day and just grabbed one when needed for drying the dishes without concern for what day of the week it was. But, I did, however, carry over a bit of "neatish" behavior through my teen years. While other teens had rooms resembling the city dump, mine was neat and organized. My closet was divided by dresses, skirts, tops and pants and in each section the clothes were organized by color. For a teenager – I was definitely not normal.

As I have gotten older, I have digressed... Fast forward 40+ years... left to my own devices, I would have a house that was livably clean but not spotless. You might find yesterdays coffee cup still on my desk and the newspaper might be thrown about the sofa. In my room there is a stack of clothes that needs to be hung up or put away. If I lie down during the day, I do not re-make the bed. My toothbrush doesn't always make it back into the holder. My bedroom slippers never make it into the closet.

I know I have a point here somewhere in the **clutter** of my mind... *In Riley World there would be a kitchen towel for every day of the week and each would have a list of tasks. He would adhere to those tasks as though they were the holy grail itself. The towels would be changed at 12:01 A.M. every single day. They would be clearly hung on some special hanger in view for all to see. There would be no deviation.*

Imagine the frustration he must

*feel when comforted with the fact that the pile of things… ***#!%** …as he calls it… accumulates on my desk and my attitude is "I'll get a round to it this week." It must cause extreme stress for him when he gives me a grocery list and I come home with only seven of the ten items. Riley lives in an absolute black and white world. I live with approximations and shades of gray with an occasional absolute thrown in.*

Riley says he has Obsessive Compulsive Disorder – I'm not so sure. The absolute routine of Riley's world has a purpose. He has told me that if he gets everything done that needs to be done, his time then becomes his own do to with as he pleases. And what he pleases is alcohol related. In his mind, it's OK to be drunk to the point of peeing your pants, if the kitchen counter is spotless. It is OK to be oblivious to the end table having rings from his beer cans if he vacuumed the floor this morning. That doesn't sound like OCD to me. It sounds more like alcoholic behavior.

There is a jagged sort of logic in his thinking. It's not one I agree with – but it belongs to him and I have no right to try to take away his thought process. As he – again – progresses towards end-stage, he needs those daily reminder towels to keep him on task because he sometimes confuses Monday with Wednesday. He has difficult remembering his self-assigned tasks and when he is to do them or even if he has already done them.

I know that part of it is the memory loss from the stroke. But I am also acutely aware that most of it is that his frontal lobe is saturated with ammonia and therefore not truly able to agree to anything for a long period of time. I also know that he finds some kind of "pay back" in creating minor difficulties for me. If he is not happy in the living arrangement, he will not let me be happy either. Or, if he makes me miserable enough, I'll send him away. **Whatever…**

I just want to give fair warning… if I see that Tuesday Towel around here, I will promptly burn it and then claim no knowledge.

I'm A Writer: My Husband Is An Alcoholic
From the Quiet Raging Waters blog posted March 5, 2015 by Wren Waters

All my life I have wanted to "be" a writer.

Or, more accurately, I have wanted to "be" a published writer for the truth is being a writer and being a published writer are two vastly different things.

To be cliche, writers are born.

Published writers are made.

And so when I was at my therapist and she asked me what my dreams were, I said,

To be a published writer.

And so she asked why don't I write.

I said I write all the time.

All.

The.

Time.

What I don't do is write and get published.

She said in this day and age, I have no excuse for not being published.

Start a blog, she said.

Does that really count as published, I said.

She assured me it counts though for me the jury is still out on that one.

What will you write about, she asked, though I suspect like a lawyer, therapists don't ask any question they don't already know the answer to.

Unfortunately, I said, I suppose the obvious.

When I majored in English as an undergrad, when I went on to get my Masters in writing, when I applied (but never went) to a PhD program in Writing, never once did I imagine that my focus would be alcoholism, much less my own husband's alcoholism. I anticipated (and for a long time wrote – or at least began) creative tomes filled with the sort of lyrical language, colorful characters and deep story lines that lets one feel justified in calling herself A Writer. I saw books piled high at the front of bookstores, while I sat signing copies and humbly accepting readers' accolades and praise.

I didn't
see myself siting alone in
front of a
keyboard 2am recounting
how the love of my life, a
man highly (HIGHLY)
respected in his field, a
man who no one (NO ONE)
in his professional circle
would ever (EVER) guess,
had spent the
evening screaming
about fucking dishes
or fucking dogs or fucking
bills or fucking noise or
fucking ANYTHING for that
matter. I didn't expect to

be writing about how there are years (YEARS) old memories that still haunt me – like racing out of the house with my then-babies at 10 pm to escape his verbal wrath.

As the tried and true adage goes, write what you know.

I didn't expect what I was going to know was slowly drowning… in the sea of my husband's alcoholism.

THANK YOU

Thank you for reading and using my book. I hope it helps in some small way to keep you sane. I am a work in progress. This book was created from my own life experiences as well as experiences of those who have contacted me. I've pulled information from every possible place where information was available. If you have suggestions or comments, please e-mail me at LindaWrites@live.com. If you find that this book doesn't meet your needs, please pass it on to someone who may find it useful.

Made in the USA
Middletown, DE
01 October 2017